Desires of the Heart
Move Forward with Power in God's Grace

Desires of the Heart
Move Forward with Power in God's Grace
Copyright © 2019 by Tulani Person

For written permission, email tulaniperson@iamtulaniperson.com

Printed in the United States of America
First Printing, 2019
ISBN: 9781075421570

Cover design by Zeljka Kojic
Editing by Lisa Whrite
Photography by Robert Bruce

This book is dedicated to

Kristian and Dayla, my beloved daughters, I dedicate this book to you because it is a testament to knowing God, Jesus, and Holy Spirit. The greatest instruction I can give as your mother is to know God.

Kristian, may you experience everything God placed in your heart.

Dayla, may this book empower you to live desires in your heart.

With Love,

Mom

Acknowledgments

There are special people in my life whose inspiration and assistance made this book possible:

To God, Jesus, and Holy Spirit, my source for living, thank you for giving me the assignment and wisdom to write this book.

To Dale Person, my loving husband, whose support allowed me to grow in wisdom. Your acts of sacrifice will never go unnoticed.

To Helen Womack, my mother, whose support inspires me to be a woman of grace. Your unconditional love gives me strength to move forward.

To Thomas Marble, my father, whose support helps me to remain focus and moving forward in life.

To Ardis Womack, my father, whose support helps me move forward in life.

To Edna Evans, my grandmother, whose encouragement during this process gave me strength. Thank you for believing in my dream.

Milton and Katrina, my brother-n-law and sister, whose support help me experience the spiritual truth of God.

Miya Banks, my sister, thank you for your wisdom and support. You inspire me in many ways.

To Phillip Johnson, my uncle, whose investment helped me move forward with this book. I salute you.

To Wanda Gilkey, my aunt, thank you for your encouragement and support to write this book.

To Anthony Joiner, my coach and strategist, whose advice helped me write this book with "a plan."

To Jennifer Yancie, my client, thank you for trusting me to serve you. Your commitment helped me write this book.

To Dr. Marsay Strozier, my collaborating partner, whose support helped me learn the process of releasing desires from the heart.

To Angie Lewis, my friend, whose support encourages me to stay in the race.

To my entire family, thank you for supporting me my entire life. I am standing on your shoulders. May I never forget the tribe who raised me.

Contents

Preface

Thank you for purchasing a copy of this book! I wrote this book with you in mind. What is your purpose? I could not answer this question for myself five years ago. Now, I can answer this question without doubts. What caused me to discover my purpose? Desires in my heart helped me to discover my purpose. This book will help you identify desires in your heart that connects you to your purpose.

I challenge you to desire what God has hidden in your heart. This starts with the desire to know God's truth about living your heart's desires. In this book, I share the true meaning of desire and how to experience your desires. It's important to read the introduction to get an understanding on how to move forward with power in God's grace. I guarantee that you will get results in your life if you read and apply what you learn in this book. I am in agreement with you that you will experience everything God placed in your heart.

With Love,

Tulani

Introduction

"You open your hand and satisfy the desires of every living thing."

Psalms 145:16 (NIV)

Are you frustrated? Is life suffocating you? Are you worn out? Do you worry? Do you wake up anxious about life circumstances? I want to share with you a true story about a man who thought life was over for him.

This man fell out of a boat while fishing with friends in Lake Michigan. He fought to keep his head above the water while using his hands to signal for help from his friends. He was thinking in his mind that life was over while experiencing the threat of drowning. His friends were yelling, "get up, get up."

The man stood up and realized he was in shallow water. Fear, doubt, and uncertainty gripped this man's mind when he fell out of the boat. He had to make one decision: to move past the fear, doubt, and uncertainty. This man had to make the decision to get up.

I lived in the waters of life circumstances. Anger, low self-esteem, people-pleasing, insecurities, depression, anxiety, and childhood wounds consumed my heart. I was coping with fear, doubt, and uncertainty about my life. I had to make the decision to get up by confronting what was blocking me from experiencing the desires of my heart. You may feel like you are drowning. The truth is you have desires in your heart for you to experience, and you have the power to confront anything that is blocking the flow.

Desire is the Starting Point to Move Forward

What is desire? Desire excites your mind on what you believe will give you satisfaction and pleasure. Desire is an internal act which influences your will to act on what you believe. Napoleon Hill said, "Desire is the starting point of all achievement, not a hope, not a wish, but a keen pulsating desire which transcends everything."

The cycle of life circumstances that don't please your mind creates an emptiness and void in your heart. This causes a person to become dissatisfied with life. Only God can guarantee a life of pleasure with a satisfied mind. Psalm 145:16 (NIV) says, "You open your hand and satisfy the desires of every living thing."

God uses desires in your heart to please you. This means that God is your source to give you pleasure with every desire in your heart. What causes God to open his hands and fulfill your desires? The knowledge of God's truth is what causes Him to fill every void in your heart. God's word is truth. Jesus said in John 17:17 (KJV), "Sanctify them by the truth; your word is truth."

The Bible is the testament of God's truth. So, it's important for you to know the truth in getting pleasure while living the desires of your heart. The desire to know God and his truth is the starting point to move beyond life circumstances.

In this book, you will receive wisdom, spiritual understanding, and knowledge of God. This will empower you to move beyond barriers that discourage you. This includes guaranteed pleasure in knowing God.

Desire is Achieved by Faith

The old faithful rotary phone had a cord that would get tangled, and it was difficult keeping it from tangling after many uses. The rotary phone was for limited movement while talking. I remember how we would move around while talking on the phone when I was a kid. Our movements stretched the cord to the point it no longer had its original form. This caused static in the phone. You knew it was time to get a new phone when you had to move the cord around to stop the static.

Circumstances will entangle you like the cord on the rotary phone. Your entanglement includes issues hidden in your heart. You're stretched to the point where you have no energy to move forward in life. This creates static that causes you to think you don't have any desires in your heart. This static blocks your frequency to hear from God.

You have a virtue, which is your power to achieve desires. This virtue is your faith. Your faith will cause God to lift you out of anything that is entangling you. You may look at your entanglement as deep water, but God looks at it as shallow water. This is why Jesus told the woman in Mark chapter 5 that her faith made her whole.

Mark 5:34 (KJV) says, "And he said unto her, Daughter, thy faith hath made thee whole; go in peace and be whole of thy plague." This woman had a blood issue for twelve years. She was entangled in debt, and her condition was getting worse. She woke up with a desire for healing and touched Jesus by faith.

You have the same faith this woman had. You may not know your desires. You need your faith to identify desires in your heart, which will make you whole. Desires are achieved by faith. Hebrews 11:1 (KJV) says, "Now, faith is the substance of things hoped for, the evidence of things not seen." You may believe that desires aren't for your experience in life. This belief may come from patterns of generational behaviors in your family. One example of generational behaviors is a family that don't finish what they start. Your desires are not based on your family background but on your faith. Faith that you have desires in your heart. Your faith can start out as the size of a mustard seed.

Matthew 17:20 (KJV) says, "And Jesus said unto them, Because of your unbelief: for verily I say unto you, If ye have faith as a grain of mustard seed, ye shall say to this mountain, Remove hence to yonder place; and it shall remove; and nothing shall be impossible unto you."

Conduct a Google image search for one mustard seed. This will help you understand the amount of faith you need to experience the desires of your heart. God created you to overcome life challenges by faith. The truth is your life journey has a way of showing how you used your faith. You overcame every life challenge by faith. 1 John 5:4 (NIV) says, "for everyone born of God overcomes the world. This is the victory that has overcome the world, even our faith."

You may have raised your children with limited resources by faith. Overcame a health challenge by faith. Graduated from college by faith. Started a career by faith. Received career promotions by faith. Started a business by faith. Whatever success you accomplished; it was achieved by faith.

Desires are Achieved with a Sound Mind

Life circumstances will keep your mind closed to moving forward. Your mind may include thoughts of regrets. This will cause you to accept life as it is.

In 2013, I suffered from major depression and anxiety. I went from confidence in my career to anxiety and fear of leaving my home. My family and I took a picture during my daughter's high school musical. My back was bent over in the picture while everyone was standing tall. Martin Luther King Jr. said, "Whenever men and women straighten their backs up, they are going somewhere, because a man can't ride your back unless it is bent." Life circumstances invaded my mind and showed in my physical posture. The posture of your mind is bent when you allow circumstances to remain in your mind. Fear, doubt, and uncertainty causes you to live without the determination to achieve desires in your heart. Desires are achieved with a sound mind. A sound mind is a mind with discipline and self-control. 2 Timothy 1:7 (KJV) says, "For God hath not given us the spirit of fear; but of power, and of love, and of a sound mind." God gave you a sound mind with wisdom, understanding, counsel, strength, and knowledge. A sound mind gives you self-control to engage your life with God's knowledge.

You would agree with me that you were focused when you accomplished goals in the past. Your thinking was clear with precise judgement to know how to move forward with plans you made by faith. A sound mind thinks and makes decisions connected to correct judgment. You experienced success with a sound mind, which is your strength. With your mind, you gained knowledge in certain areas of your life. You learned how to be humble. You trust your instincts when making decisions. You know the power of patience when you need it. You have extra strengths in your mind. So, it is clear you are a person of faith and have a sound mind to discover and fulfill the desires of your heart.

My Story

I desired to go to college while attending high school. My high school grades were below average, and my ACT score was a fifteen. I applied to one college, Eastern Michigan University, by faith. I was accepted and successfully completed my freshman year.

I returned home for the summer and desired a car. I believed God for a Saturn. I was told I was aiming too high to have faith for a newer model car at the time. I had the desire to pursue that particular car. I got a summer job while searching for a Saturn. I returned to school for Fall 1994 with a 1992 Saturn. I graduated from college by faith. I returned home pregnant. I had no clue about my future. By faith, I started a job at Head Start. I gave birth to my beautiful daughter, Kristian, with every need being met.

In 1999, I was blessed to start my career of 18 years by faith. I was able to provide financial support for my daughter as a single mother. One of the most exciting times of my life was the joy I felt when I unlocked the door to my new home as a first-time homebuyer.

In 2013, I was no longer single and married my loving husband, Dale. We welcomed our precious daughter, Dayla, in 2015. Every achievement started with a desire. I pursued every desire by faith with discipline. My strengths helped me be the person I was in the past and who I am now. There was one thing that was inconsistent during my achievements. My desire for God was up and down. I desired God when I needed something but lacked affection for God when life was going well. My relationship with God was out of harmony.

My Life Became Empty

I hit a point in my life when my heart was empty. I achieved the "American Dream," but life no longer had meaning to me. I achieved milestones but was in deep sorrow. My life spiraled out of control when I experienced depression. I entered the reality that I didn't know who I was. I experienced silent frustration and dreaded living. I knew if I didn't gain control of the negative emotions that dominated my day, I would regress in living. My heart was deeply discouraged.

I chose the path to seek God. I wanted to know the truth about Tulani. I needed to know who God created me to be. I sought God and received the truth about me. This was a process. The biggest hurdle I faced was discouragement. Discouragement is a wall that everyone hits at some point in their life. Discouragement doesn't discriminate. It attacks all races, ages, and genders.

What Do You Do When You Are Discouraged?

How do you respond to life when you are discouraged? Discouragement is an indicator that you have unfulfilled desires in your heart. Discouragement keeps people from receiving inspiration and knowledge.

In Exodus Chapter 3, God assigned Moses to lead the Israelites out of Egypt. Later, God sent Moses to tell the Israelites that He will set them free in Exodus Chapter 6. Exodus 6:9 (NIV) says, "Moses reported this to the Israelites, but they did not listen to him because of their discouragement and harsh labor." The Israelites became discouraged while suffering harsh labor from Pharaoh, King of Egypt. They went from having plenty of resources to forced slavery with nothing.

I want to pause and ask you to think about the circumstances in your life that caused you to be discouraged. You may feel oppressed. Your life may have been great. You experienced abundance in your life. Now, your life is filled with dread, disappointment, and discouragement. The Israelites cried out to God for help. God heard their cries and remembered his covenant with their forefathers. God prepared Moses to be their leader. The Israelites did not receive Moses because of discouragement. Discouragement comes from sorrow. Sorrow is uneasiness/pain of the mind. The Israelites' minds were in pain because of slavery. You experience pain in your mind when life brings unexpected challenges. You experience pain in your mind when you experience any type of loss. Any type of loss creates life setbacks and discouragement. You may have prayed and cried out to God for help. I want you to know that God heard your prayers and cries. God uses inspiration and knowledge to get you out of situations. Has discouragement caused you to doubt God and his knowledge?

This book is to help you shift your mind from discouragement to taking pleasure in God. **Remember: Discouragement is an indicator of unfulfilled desires in your heart.** Only God can fulfill your heart desires. Psalm 37:4 (KJV) says, "Delight thyself also in the Lord: and he shall give thee the desires of thine heart." Delight is a high degree of pleasure, or satisfaction of mind. The weapon for discouragement is to have a high degree of pleasure for God every day. Delight includes taking satisfaction in the truth of who God created you to be. This opens God's hand to fulfill your desires. God desires for you to seek him to discover who you are in His image and likeness.

Take Pleasure in Being Made in God's Image

Genesis 1:27 (KJV) says, "So God created man in his own image, in the image of God created he him; male and female created he them." Your desires are revealed when you take pleasure in being who you were created to be in God's image and likeness. First, it is important to understand that Jesus is the image of God. Colossians 1:15 (NIV) says, "The Son is the image of the invisible God, the firstborn over all creation."

Image is a representation or similitude of any person or thing. We are to reflect Jesus nature as believers in Jesus Christ. This means we are to think, act, and use our emotions like Jesus. This is a truth you must live by daily to experience desires in your heart. Your old nature is dead, and your life is hidden in Christ. Colossians 3:3 (KJV) says, "For ye are dead, and your life is hid with Christ in God." What is the image of God? The image of God is a reflection of what God thinks.

Another definition of image is a representation of anything to the mind. This boils down to what you think.

You are literally what you think. We as humans are what we think. Proverbs 23:7 (KJV) says, "For as he thinketh in his heart, so is he:" James Allen said it best when he said, "A man is literally what he thinks, his character being the complete sum of all his thoughts." You were given a mind to think like God. It's a pleasure to know that through Jesus, you have access to God's thoughts. The same thoughts he had when he created you in His image and likeness.

Take Pleasure in God

There are three truths to put into action to take pleasure in God and to experience desires in your heart. The three truths are resting in God, receiving the mind of Christ, and growing in wisdom. The following are descriptions of each:

1. **Resting in God:** Rest by learning Christ's teachings to apply in every area of your life. This includes knowing how to implement spiritual and natural laws that govern life. Jesus said, **"Are you tired? Worn out? Burned out on religion? Come to me. Get away with me, and you'll recover your life. I'll show you how to take a real rest. Walk with me and work with me—watch how I do it. Learn the unforced**

rhythms of grace. I won't lay anything heavy or ill-fitting on you. Keep company with me, and you'll learn to live freely and lightly." Matthew 11:28-30 (The Message)* You will know how to rest when you receive Christ's teachings.

2. **Receive the Mind of Christ:** Allow Jesus' thoughts to be your thoughts. This includes a strategy to use your mind like Jesus used his. Philippians 2:5 (KJV) says, **"Let this mind be in you, which was also in Christ Jesus:"**

3. **Grow in Wisdom:** Grow spiritually in God's wisdom. Jesus grew in wisdom to fulfill his mission. We are to grow spiritually in wisdom by law. You progress in your soul (mind, will, and emotions) when you grow in wisdom. Luke 2:52 (NIV) says, **"And Jesus grew in wisdom and stature, and in favor with God and man."** Growth is required to represent the fullness of God's image.

I will share God's truth and strategies for you to experience the desires of your heart.
God created you. Jesus redeemed you. The Holy Spirit will guide you into your truth. The Holy Spirit is the spirit of God that gives you guidance. Ask the Holy Spirit to give

you spiritual understanding and guidance as you continue to read this book. Jesus said in John 16:13 (KJV), "Howbeit when he, the Spirit of truth, is come, he will guide you into all truth: for he shall not speak of himself; but whatsoever he shall hear, that shall he speak: and he will shew you things to come."

Get an Idea from God

An idea from God will move you forward. My client, Jennifer Yancie received an idea from God to create toddler training pants with organic materials. She made a prototype of the training pants, but placed it on the shelf for several years. She shared her idea with me and explained how long the prototype was on the shelf. I challenged Jennifer to "breath life" into her product by moving forward with it. Jennifer registered for my first class. She consistently attended my workshops and group sessions to receive the knowledge needed to move forward with power in God's grace. At the time of writing this book, Jennifer's product, EZ Doez It, is being sold at Macy's in San Francisco, California. Jennifer's idea from God empowered her to move forward. God has an idea for you to experience a life of freedom. How often do ideas pop up in your mind? In Chapter 9, I share truths to living your vision from God.

See Yourself Free Through Jesus

You are free in Jesus Christ! Galatians 5:1 (NIV) says, "Stand fast therefore in the liberty wherewith Christ hath made us free, and be not entangled again with the yoke of bondage." You must see yourself free to experience the desires of your heart. Christ has given you the freedom to live your life in Him without limits. You are free!

Elizabeth Keckley was born into slavery. She experienced physical and sexual abuse during the thirty years of being a slave. For example, she was beaten as a child for accidentally tipping over her slave master's baby in a cradle. She was often told by her owners that she was not worth salt. Ms. Keckley's Mother taught her how to sew. She became a skilled seamstress as a slave. Keckley became a reputable seamstress among affluent women in St. Louis, Missouri. She had a desire and saw herself free while being the sole provider for her slave master. She cared for her slave master's household of seventeen people for two years and five months.

Keckley asked her slave master if she could buy her freedom, and after several requests, her slave master agreed for $1,200. Later, Elizabeth Keckley became the seamstress at the White House. She served Mary Todd Lincoln, wife of Abraham Lincoln.

Ms. Keckley had a vision to be free before she experienced freedom. She said, "Free, free! What a glorious ring to the word. Free! The bitter heart-struggle was over. Free! The soul could go out to heaven and to God with no chains to clog its flight or pull it down. Free! The earth wore a brighter look, and the very stars seemed to sing with joy. Yes, free! Free by the laws of man and the smile of God." Do see yourself free to live the desires of your heart?

Own Your Truth

Living the desires of your heart is about owning the truth of God's word. God's word is truth. Jesus said in John 17:17 (KJV), **"Sanctify them through thy truth: thy word is truth."** Sanctify means to be separate. God desires for you to live sanctified by his word. You must ask yourself, "Do you believe his word as your truth to live by? Your beliefs drive your behavior. If you believe his word to be your truth, you will take action to live the desires of your heart.

Owning your truth starts with making a choice to engage your life the way God created you. You will not get results in your life by just reading this book. Discovering and living the desires of your heart starts with making a choice to live by the truth of God's word. The following are four steps to making a choice:

1. **Commit to the process:** Discovering your desires is a process with a commitment. This includes committing to spiritual growth. Truth is revealed to you as you grow spiritually. This is a process because your natural mind doesn't know the desires God placed in your heart. Only the Spirit of God can reveal them to you. **1 Corinthians 2:9 (NIV) says, "What no eye has seen, what no ear has heard, and what no human mind has conceived the things God has prepared for those who love him."** Your natural mind doesn't know what God has for you. They are hidden pleasures.

2. **Establish your faith:** Faith is believing God's word without evidence, of what you can't see with your natural eyes. For example, you can't see Jesus with your natural eyes. Your faith is needed to receive all the desires hidden in your heart. Hebrews 11:1 (KJV)

says, "**Now, faith is the substance of things hoped for, the evidence of things not seen.**" Faith is connected to what you do not see hidden in your heart.

3. **Move forward:** God is in the business of restoring your soul for you to experience pleasure in living. Your choice should include your focus: moving forward. Philippians 3:13-14 (KJV) says, "**Brethren, I count not myself to have apprehended: but this one thing I do, forgetting those things which are behind, and reaching forth unto those things which are before, ¹⁴ I press toward the mark for the prize of the high calling of God in Christ Jesus.**" This means whatever happened in your past doesn't matter. What matters is what God planned for you in your future.

4. **Expect results:** Expect results while discovering and living your desires. Your expectation leads to results you desire to experience. You are making the choice knowing that God has an expected end for you. Jeremiah 29:11 (NIV) says, "**For I know the plans I have for you,**" declares the LORD, "**plans to prosper you and not to harm you, plans to give you hope**

and a future." God plans for you includes results full of his goodness.

God approved you to live the desires of your heart. He created you to follow his blueprint to experience your best life. He created the universe by faith. Hebrews 11:3 (NIV) says, "By faith, we understand that the universe was formed at God's command, so that what is seen was not made out of what was visible." God gave you faith to expect desires to flow from your heart. Now, it's important for you to know how to produce the desires from your heart by taking pleasure in seeking God.

Jesus said in Matthew 6:33 (KJV), "But seek ye first the kingdom of God, and his righteousness; and all these things shall be added unto you." Seeking God's kingdom includes resting while having the mind of Christ and growing in wisdom. You made the choice to live the desires of your heart. Now you are ready to discover and live the desires hidden in your heart.

Prayer of Salvation

If you have not received Jesus in your heart, you may receive him as your Savior and Lord with a prayer of salvation. Romans 10:9 (NIV) says, "If you declare with your mouth, "Jesus is Lord," and believe in your heart that God raised him from the dead, you will be saved."

Say aloud the following prayer of salvation:
God, I confess Jesus as my Lord. I acknowledge and repent of my sins. I believe in my heart that you raised Jesus from the dead, and now I am saved. Thank you for the gift of salvation! In Jesus Name, Amen.

Welcome to the Kingdom of God!

Chapter 1

Desires of the Heart

"Take delight in the LORD, and he will give you the desires of your heart."

Psalms 37:4 (NIV)

Do you ever get an urge or push that you should be doing something? It may be to improve a specific area in your life or to be a better person. The urge or push are desires in your heart. Desire influences your will to act. It's an internal force in your heart that pushes you to act. In other words, God uses desires to influence you to take action.

Picture a beautiful home. Every room in the house is breathtaking, but there is a problem. Water is seeping through the cracks of the foundation. The owner is aware but decides to take care of the water cracks when time permits. Now, the foundation of the home is severely damaged. Why? The owner didn't take quick action to repair the cracks. I used this illustration to explain how God's grace seeks to connect to desires in your heart.

What Is God's Grace?

One definition of God's grace is divine influence on the heart. Hebrews 4:7 (KJV) says, "To day, if ye will hear his voice, harden not your hearts." God's desire is to influence your heart. Remember the day you accepted Jesus into your heart. God's spirit was touching your heart. God's grace touched your emotions and influenced you to confess Jesus as your Lord and Savior. It was God's grace that connected to your desire to receive salvation. God's grace saved you. Ephesians 2:8-9 (KJV) says, "For by grace are ye saved through faith; and that not of yourselves: it is the gift of God: [9] Not of works, lest any man should boast."

God's grace is not based on your income, social status, or what you've achieved. It's God's unmerited favor and love towards you. God's grace is a privilege, advantage, and benefit to you as a believer in Christ. It's available to you by faith. Romans 5:2 (KJV) says, "By whom also we have access by faith into this grace wherein we stand, and rejoice in hope of the glory of God." Jesus is full of grace. Jesus is the only person that can give you God's grace. 1 Corinthians 1:4 (KJV) says, "I thank my God always on your behalf, for the grace of God which is given you by Jesus Christ;" I am grateful for God's grace.

"God's desire is to influence your heart."

God's grace moves with influence over your heart through righteousness by Jesus Christ. Righteousness is being in right standing with God. Jesus gave his life so you can be in correct standing with God. God doesn't look at your mishaps, flaws, nor bad habits. God sees you as the apple of his eye, admiring the way he created you. God sees himself when he looks at you. He sees his vision for your life. God rejoices over his plans for your life. He takes pleasure in his mind about the talents he's gifted you to use. Sin is anything that separates you from God.

According to Romans 6:14, God's grace gives you dominion over sin. You have power over anything that tries to separate you from God. You have dominion to experience the abundant life Jesus provided for you. This includes eternal life by grace through righteousness by Jesus.

God's Grace Comes with Eternal Life

Eternal life is a life that continues without stopping. It includes life after death on earth. It began the day you accepted Jesus in your heart. Do you feel stuck? Eternal life gives you the momentum to live without being stuck in life. Eternal life has the momentum to move you past anything that robs you of moving forward in life. Think of the Energizer Bunny.

In the Energizer battery commercials, the pink mechanical toy rabbit never stops running. The toy rabbit moves by the Energizer battery that allows it to keep going and going and going. Eternal life gives you the energy to keep going and going. It is a power that moves you past anything that opposes the truth of who you are.

"Eternal life has the momentum to move you past anything that robs you of moving forward in life."

Jesus defines eternal life as knowing him and God. Jesus said in John 17:3 (KJV), "And this is life eternal, that they might know thee the only true God, and Jesus Christ, whom thou hast sent."

Jesus empowered you with the responsibility to have knowledge about him and God. This involves knowing who God is and who he created you to be. Knowing from the Bible who Jesus is. Having the knowledge on how to live your life from God's word. Knowledge is the key to knowing how to experience eternal life on earth. Hosea 4:6 (KJV) says, "My people are destroyed for lack of knowledge:" Lack of knowledge blocks you from experiencing eternal life. Your understanding of God and Jesus is what keeps your life in motion. This guarantees power to move forward in God's grace. This knowledge comes from the mountain of the Lord.

The Mountain of the Lord

In the Book of Isaiah, Isaiah prophesied about the mountain of the Lord's temple. Isaiah acknowledged the Lord's temple would be established in the last days. Isaiah Chapter 2 provides details of Isaiah's prophecy.

Isaiah 2:2 (NIV) says, "In the last days the mountain of the LORD's temple will be established as the highest of the mountains; it will be exalted above the hills, and all nations will stream to it."

The mountain of the Lord is a place to get knowledge about God. It's a place to receive God's teachings, instructions, and guidance for your life. Isaiah said people of all nations would go to God to learn his thoughts, ways, and plans for their lives. Isaiah 2:3 (NIV) says, "Many peoples will come and say, 'Come, let us go up to the mountain of the LORD, to the temple of the God of Jacob. He will teach us his ways, so that we may walk in his paths.' The law will go out from Zion, the word of the LORD from Jerusalem."

You are in a time when God's instructions are needed for every area of your life. Think of being you. It's hard to wake up every day to get motivated. Next, you are fighting procrastination all day. You challenge yourself to overcome bad habits. You struggle to break them. Oh, the thoughts that roll in your mind that you are not good enough. How do you cleanse your mind from negative thinking? Do you need God's instructions? God desires to give you the secret to having a successful life. The secrets are revealed by knowing Him and Jesus.

Where is the Lord's temple? I have been there. This is my hangout spot. I get my peace, joy, motivation, plans, strength to develop good habits, etc. in the Lord's temple. The Lord's temple is YOU! You are the Lord's temple. 1 Corinthians 3:16 (KJV) says, "Know ye not that ye are the temple of God, and that the Spirit of God dwelleth in you?" God dwells within you to give you knowledge. The Bible gives signs to identify the last days. God promised he will pour out his spirit on all people in the last days. Acts 2:17 (NIV) says, "In the last days, God says, I will pour out my Spirit on all people." God desires to live in you to have a divine influence on your heart. This is God's way of pouring out his spirit on you.

God Wants Your Heart

It's God's desire for you to have a relationship with him. He wants all your heart in the relationship. In Acts Chapter 11, The people of the Church in Antioch experienced the Holy Spirit when Peter gave them a message from God. They received salvation as their lives changed instantly. Barnabas came to Antioch to witness the news he heard from Jerusalem. He saw God's grace in their lives and encouraged the Church in Antioch to stay connected to God with their heart. Acts 11:23 (KJV) says, "Who, when he came, and had seen the grace of God, was glad, and exhorted them all, that with purpose of heart they would cleave unto the Lord." God's grace has a divine influence on you when you connect to him with your heart. How do you connect your heart to God? You connect to God by desiring God with all your heart. This is how God's grace influences your heart. Jesus said in Matthew 22:37 (KJV), "Jesus said unto him, 'Thou shalt love the Lord thy God with all thy heart, and with all thy soul, and with all thy mind." The desire of the heart is to love God with all your heart. This is the first and great commandment Jesus acknowledged in Matthew 22:38.

Establish Your Heart in God's Grace

I honor Pastors and Ministers who teach God's word. I recognize they are humans and messengers of God. I must admit that I use to put their opinions on being a Christian before God. God gave me a gift to dance, specifically to worship music. I was in my twenties when I started dancing. It was my way of expressing my love for God, but I stopped because it wasn't acknowledged in many churches.

As a certified speaker, trainer, and coach, I overcame the criticism of being in the personal growth industry. God's word confirmed my calling in this industry. There were several occasions when I heard Pastors and Ministers speak against "self-help." My heart was established in God's grace to know what I was called to do. You will know your calling when your heart is established in God's grace.

Hebrews 13:9 (KJV) says, "Be not carried about with divers and strange doctrines. For it is a good thing that the heart be established with grace; not with meats, which have not profited them that have been occupied therein." Adapting your heart to God's doctrine keeps you connected to God's grace. The Latin root word for doctrine is to teach. Jesus taught God's doctrine. John 7:16 (KJV) says, "Jesus answered them, and said, 'My doctrine is not mine, but his that sent me." Jesus' teachings to his disciples were from God. Your heart is established in God's grace when you learn Jesus' teachings. God instructed me to join the John Maxwell Team as I was learning Jesus' teachings. This came from God's divine influence on my heart.

You are a spirit. Your heart receives what comes from your spirit when your heart is established in God's grace. Your heart isn't your physical heart. Your heart is your mind. It's your conscience. Take a moment and picture a chair in your mind. Your heart is like a chair that provides a seat for the following:

1. The seat of your passion and affection: Your love, joy, excitement, etc.
2. The seat of your will: Your intention and determination when taking action
3. The seat of your understanding: Includes six intellectual faculties:
   - Perception
   - Imagination
   - Intuition
   - Memory
   - Reason
   - Will

Your soul is your mind, will, and emotions. Your heart is interconnected with your soul. God uses your heart to produce spiritual activity and growth. This occurs when you know God. Knowing God includes having a relationship with him. I know who is walking up or down the stairs in my home. I am able to move around because I know who is in the house with me. I am able to identify when my husband or daughters use the stairs because I know them; I have a relationship with them. You know when God is influencing your heart when you have a relationship with him. This including knowing when God is inspiring, speaking, or guiding your heart. This is why it's essential for your heart to remain fixed on God with your whole desire. This takes discipline and focus. Your heart is neutral. It conforms to what you give attention to. Ralph Waldo Emerson said, "Beware what you set your heart upon. For it surely shall be yours."

Your heart/soul is the center of your being. It's a receiver that accepts whatever you give attention to. Your heart/soul will collect God's thoughts and ways from your spirit. This includes spiritual understanding of God's truth. Your mind expands and expresses God's thoughts as you keep your heart towards him.

Your heart/soul receives from your five senses. The five senses are sight, touch, taste, smell, and hear. For example, your heart receives what you view on social media. Your heart will ignore God when you give full attention to your five senses. You can't identify what's best for you from your heart alone. God said in Jeremiah 17:9 (NIV), "The heart is deceitful above all things and beyond cure. Who can understand it?" You must be intentional to connect your heart/soul to your spirit. This happens when you desire a relationship with God. The following are three truths to establishing your heart in God's grace:

1. The Desire for God to Remain in Your Mind
Your heart is the place God chose to dwell Deuteronomy 18:6 (KJV) says, "And if a Levite come from any of thy gates out of all Israel, where he sojourned, **and come with all the desire of his mind unto the place which the Lord shall choose**;" Desire God's influence to dwell in your mind.

2. The Desire to Know God's Divine Nature in Your Soul
Keep in your memory what you know about God's nature and character. Isaiah 26:8 (KJV) says, "Yea, in the way of thy judgments, O Lord, have we waited for thee; **the**

desire of our soul is to thy name, and to the remembrance of thee." This helps your soul remember the truth of what you know about God during adversity.

3. The Desire to Hold God in High Esteem with Reverence and Respect

Fearing God is having reverence for God. This keeps your heart open to receive from God. Nehemiah 1:11 (KJV) says, "O Lord, I beseech thee, let now thine ear be attentive to the prayer of thy servant, and to the prayer of thy servants **who desire to fear thy name**:" Your desire to reverence God allows your soul to have pleasure and prosper in God.

God's Grace Connects with Your "Being"

Desire is an excitement of the mind. God's grace excites your mind when you make room for him in your heart. Your spirit is the foundation of who you were created to be. God's grace seeks expression from your spirit to your heart. God attached the desire for you to live in his image and likeness when he created you. Genesis 1:27 (KJV) says, "So God created man in his own image, in the image of God created he him; male and female created he them." God wants you to desire to be who he created you to be in his image and likeness. In addition, God commanded you to be fruitful, multiply, and replenish the earth. This is a call to action from the desires of the heart.

Genesis 1:28 (KJV) says, "And God blessed them, and God said unto them, 'Be fruitful, and multiply, and replenish the earth, and subdue it: and have dominion." This command includes producing God's plans for your life. God was speaking to the spirit of human beings to desire (take action) to live his plans for their lives. Jeremiah 29:11 (NIV) says, "For I know the plans I have for you," declares the Lord, "plans to prosper you and not to harm you, plans to give you hope and a future." You are a spirit that possesses a soul, which is your mind, will, and emotions and live in a body. God's grace connects with your desire for "being." God's grace influences your heart when you take action on "being":

1. Who you were created to be in God's image (Genesis 1:27)

2. God's plans for your life (Jeremiah 29:11)

Your desires expand into other areas of your life when you take action on being who you were created to be.

Think of a time when you were a child. You desired to live your life to the fullest. You had big dreams that you were going to live, but life happened. You experienced unfavorable circumstances, rejections, and setbacks. This caused your desires to diminish. You may have suppressed your desires because of fear, doubt, and uncertainty. Some people may have viewed your desires as pipe dreams or wishes, delusions that'll never come true. You may have made the decision to settle for whatever came your way. You may be the person that never had the opportunity to dream. You experienced a childhood that was traumatic for you.

Whatever your past may reflect, you have a desire "to be" more than who you are now. Everyone wants to feel appreciated and recognized in life. If you are saying, "that's not me," I want you to check your pulse to see if you are living.

It's human nature to want to be recognized in life. Human nature is the way we naturally think, act, or feel. You were created in love, and love seeks significance and appreciation. Every day, God's grace is attempting to influence you "to be" more. This influence is connected to you being who you were created to be. The issue is when you don't take action on the desire to be the person you were created to be, you become frustrated. You frustrate God's grace too. Galatians 2:21 (KJV), **"I do not frustrate the grace of God: for if righteousness come by the law, then Christ is**

dead in vain." This causes you to go through the circle of life without experiencing the truth of who you are.

You lose sight of who you were created to be when you don't take action on living this desire "to be" more. James 1:23-24 (NIV) says, "Anyone who listens to the word but does not do what it says is like someone who looks at his face in a mirror [24] and, after looking at himself, goes away and immediately forgets what he looks like." You are wired to live in God's image. Your image becomes distorted when you don't live God's desires for your life. You cannot see yourself the way God sees you.

The Latin meaning for distort means twisted apart. Distort is defined as being pulled or twisted out of shape. You were created to live in harmony/oneness with God from your spirit, soul (mind, will, & emotions), and body. Your spirit, soul, and body are twisted apart when your image is distorted. Have you ever heard a musical group sing out of harmony? You cannot enjoy the song. This is the same as you not taking action to live your desires. You can't enjoy your life living apart from God; this creates a distorted view of God, yourself, and life. You can't experience the real reason for living. Instead, you live in the cycle of sorrow.

The Cycle of Sorrow

Sorrow is the uneasiness or pain of mind. Sorrow comes when you experience any type of loss in life. A loss of happiness, frustrated hopes, or causes of grief. Sorrow is the consequence God gave to mankind. This is a result of Adam following Eve by eating from the tree of the knowledge of good and evil. Genesis 2:17 (KJV) says, "But of the tree of the knowledge of good and evil, thou shalt not eat of it: for in the day that thou eatest thereof thou shalt surely die." God's instruction to Adam was a spiritual law Adam was to live by. When this law was violated, Adam was separated from God. This is the ultimate sin. Adam was separated from being the person God created him to be and from God's original plans for his life. Adam and Eve's choice to violate God's spiritual law changed the nature of human beings.

Their actions distorted and polluted our human nature. Adam's actions created consequences for human beings. One of God's consequences for human beings who live separate from him is sorrow. Genesis 3:17 (KJV) says, "And unto Adam he said, Because thou hast hearkened unto the voice of thy wife, and hast eaten of the tree, of which I commanded thee, saying, Thou shalt not eat of it: cursed is the ground for thy sake; in sorrow shalt thou eat of it all the days of thy life." Sorrow is an indicator that your life is not in oneness with God. You were created to remain connected to God by depending on him. God created you to rely on him in how you think, how you act, and how you feel. Here are some symptoms of sorrow (not all) when you don't depend on God to be who you were created to be:

- Dread life including your career, relationships, etc.
- Restlessness
- Seek pleasures to satisfy the void/emptiness in your heart
- Wander from one action to another with no results
- Silent frustration
- Questioning God's nature with doubt and uncertainty

Sorrow is a never-ending cycle that comes with dread. I dreaded going to work daily. I went to work with my focus on the upcoming weekend. I had Sunday night blues knowing I had to go to work on Monday morning. I didn't know that I was driving to work daily in silent frustration. I commuted to work with no productive thinking, just living a daily routine without being who I was created to be.

I became aware that I was living a life of dread when I went to hear Bishop TD Jakes speak at Lakewood Church in Houston, Texas on May 25, 2014.

That day, I woke up excited. I knew God was going to impart something into my spirit. I anticipated hearing Bishop Jakes' message like a child waiting for Christmas. I didn't know his word would cause a shift in my mindset to desire to be the person I was created to be.

Bishop Jakes started his sermon. Nothing could keep me from receiving his message as I listened with joy in my heart. My mind shifted when he asked the audience questions. He asked questions as if he was throwing baseballs at me at the speed of 90 mph. These questions quickened my spirit to know God needed me just as much as I needed God. He asked the audience, "Are you tired of your daily routine? Are you living with purpose?" I responded with tears. I entered the awareness that my dread and frustration were indicators of an empty heart. I thought my career was my place of recognition, promotion, and retirement. My career became a place of dread as my years of service increased. I was grateful for my job but dreaded going to work daily. I swept under the rug my feelings while giving 100% attention to my job. I was suffocating the desires hidden in my heart.

Gallup, a polling consulting firm, released their State of the American Workplace study. They found Seventy Percent of Americans are not engaged with their careers. This study provides several reasons why. One reason is Americans aren't satisfied with their employer.

Jim Clifton, CEO of Gallup offers six solutions in this study. One out of the six solutions is for organizations to help their employees recognize their God-given talents. A person not satisfied with their employer indicates unfulfilled desires in their heart. You break the cycle of sorrow by seeking pleasure in God. This is a pill you must swallow to break the cycle in your life.

The Benefits of Depending on God

God's grace is favor that will empower you to live in the fullness of God's image and likeness. You are God's favorite. I was in a store and hesitated to tell a person what I did for a living. I drove home questioning why I waited to answer the person. I hesitated to tell the person because I didn't feel gifted on that day. I was having a bad hair day with no make-up and tired. I was in my feelings. You don't see immediate results when you come into the knowledge of who you were created to be. You deal with your realities while expanding your mind in God's wisdom. We are familiar with our five senses. It's easy to respond to life based on our feelings. We are quick to judge ourselves. God doesn't hold against you the moments when you don't feel your best. God's approves of you when you are feeling good and bad. Every day, God sees himself when he sees you.

The benefit of God's favor toward you is being like him with his power and provision.

Michael Jordan, one of the greatest basketball players, didn't favor anyone to be like him. He didn't share his secrets to having basketball intelligence. Few basketball players know the process of being great like Michael Jordan. God desires to share with you all his secrets to being great.

God favored you to be great. The seed of greatness on the inside of you is having the favor to be like God. God's grace is your benefit to be a small case g. To be a god. Jesus said in John 10:34 (KJV), **"...Is it not written in your law, I said, Ye are gods?"**

The benefits of depending on God is to use his name and authority:

- To think like God
- Talk like God
- Act like God
- Create like God
- Love like God
- Imagine like God
- Serve like God

God granted you favor to have access to his nature. He gives you the secrets to be like him when you desire him. God, the creator of the universe, desires to give you the secrets to prosper your life. Psalm 20:4 (NIV) says, "May he give you the desire of your heart and make all your plans succeed." God has secrets that will empower you to prosper in every area of your life.

You cannot go through the process of living desires in your heart without God. Negative emotions attempt daily to dominate your day. Leaving a cycle of sorrow is a process. This comes with renewing your mind and growing in the knowledge of God. One word to illustrate leaving the cycle of sorrow is rhythm. Your physical heart beats in rhythm.

The heart of your mind was designed to operate in rhythm with God's grace.

This is the battleground of your mind. Negative emotions that dominate your life are on autopilot. Anger was a negative emotion that dominated my life for several years. I would explode when anything agitated my mind. Anger would cause me to shut down mentally.

When I was angry about something, I made decisions that didn't reflect God's thoughts nor ways. My choices didn't reflect who I was created to be. My opportunity to allow anger to dominate my day kept me unproductive. I was living my life in my strength. My strength couldn't produce the desires of my heart. God's grace is your strength to overcome any negative emotions that dominate your day. Negative emotions are weaknesses in your life. 2 Corinthians 12:9 (KJV) says, "And he said unto me, My grace is sufficient for thee: for my strength is made perfect in weakness." Most gladly, therefore, will I rather glory in my infirmities, that the power of Christ may rest upon me." God's grace is your strength to overcome your weaknesses, including negative emotions. This is a benefit of depending on God.

Let's play the "what if" game! What if God told you to open a school and you've never been an educator? What if

God told you to create a children's cartoon and you don't know how to draw? What if God said to host a talk show and you have a fear of public speaking? What if God told you to open a recording studio and you don't have recording technology? What if God said to run for a political office and you don't know anything about political science? What if God told you to become a philanthropist and you have no money in your bank account?

What did God instruct you to do? Any desire connected to God's grace is a tree of life. Proverbs 13:12 (KJV) says, "Hope deferred maketh the heart sick: but when the desire cometh, it is a tree of life." The tree of life is your source for being who you are created to be. This tree is God's covenant to give you the knowledge to be successful without sorrow. You have access to the tree of life when you act on what God instructs you to do. God will give you the knowledge to do something beyond human reasoning. In your mind, it's impossible to do what God instructs you to do. In God's mind, his instructions come with knowledge. You can be who you were created to be with the intellect to do what God instructs you to do. The tree of life allows God's word to be planted in your heart while receiving counsel from him. God's counsel will give the intelligence needed to act on what he instructed you to do even when you are weak.

God instructed me to coordinate a mentoring group at the high school I was assigned to. God gave me this instruction while I was experiencing depression and anxiety. I cried during the first week of my assignment. I didn't know the condition of public schools. I was awakened by the problems students face daily.

My first week, I met students who were homeless, prostituting, hungry, and depressed. I prayed and asked God where the church was. God's response was clear. He reminded me that I was the church.

I arranged for a church to mentor a group of students weekly. I participated in the mentoring sessions. I observed and connected with the students. I noticed how my intelligence was linked to human behavior and potential. God was showing me how we are wired in his image and likeness.

I started to learn about the law of rhythm before I knew it was a universal law. This led me to speak at a trade school. My topic was "Live your truth, create your vision." I created content from what I learned and experienced from the mentoring group. God instructed me to join the John Maxwell Team in October 2015. God's call to action for me to coordinate the mentoring group put me on a path to discover the desires of my heart. I entered the process recognizing who I was created to be and God's plans for my life. You will get the benefits from the tree of life by desiring what God instructs you to do.

Desires of The Heart

Napoleon Hill said, "Desire is the starting point of all achievement." He discovered this truth through research. He researched more than five-hundred wealthy people for twenty years. God uses desire as your starting point of achievement.

I want to make it clear again that the starting point/foundation of your desire is the following:

- Being who you were created to be in God's image (Genesis 1:27)
- Living God's plans for your life (Jeremiah 29:11)

God never intended for your desire of life pleasures to be more than your desire to love him with all of your heart. Do you have a hunger for God? Do you have a craving to remain in right standing with God? Jesus said in Matthew 5:6 (KJV), "Blessed are those who hunger and thirst for righteousness, for they will be filled." Hunger and thirst are descriptions for desire. Righteousness is being in right standing with God. God will fill you when you desire to stay in right standing with him. You will be filled with God's divine nature. This includes the intellect to live your life. God will give you instructions when you hunger for his righteousness.

Desires of the heart are not based on if you have the money to act on an idea from God or you living in the right market to grow your business. Your bad habits, failures, nor past has nothing to do with the criteria of God giving you the desires in your heart. God qualifies you when you hunger, thirst, and have a burning desire for him.

This includes your mind taking satisfaction in four truths:

1. God
2. God's word
3. Who God created you to be
4. Discovering God's plans for your life

Having a hunger and satisfaction for truth in your mind activates the desires in your heart. Proverbs 13:19 (KJV) says, **"The desire accomplished is sweet to the soul...."** This hangs on your desire to love God with all your heart.

Chapter 1 Summary:

- Desire is an internal force in your heart that pushes you to take action
- God uses desires to influence you to take action
- One definition of God's grace is a divine influence on the heart
- God's grace exercises influence over your heart through righteousness by Jesus Christ
- Jesus gave you the responsibility to have knowledge about him and God
- God desires to dwell in your spirit, while having a divine influence on your heart
- Your heart is established in God's grace when you learn Jesus' teachings

- The desire of the heart is to love God with all your heart

- **God uses the desire to influence you to take action on the following:**

  1. To be who you were created to be in his image and likeness (Genesis 1:27)
  2. To live his plans for your life (Jeremiah 29:11)

- Your heart is where spiritual activity and growth comes

- **Your heart is like a chair that provides a seat for the following:**

    1. The seat for your passion and affection: Your love, joy, excitement, etc.
    2. The Seat for Your Will: Your intention and determination when taking action
    3. The Seat for Your Understanding: This includes six intellectual faculties:

        1. Perception
        2. Imagination
        3. Intuition
        4. Memory
        5. Reason
        6. Will

- You break the cycle of sorrow by taking pleasure in God
- Having a hunger and satisfaction for truth in your mind activates the desires in your heart.

A Call To Action

God reveals his truth for you to take action. God has a strategy for every truth he desires for you to experience. Sorrow helps you identify that you need God's knowledge in your life.

What part of your life gives you sorrow?

Your acknowledgment of sorrow moves you toward discovering and living the desires in your heart. The action step you must take after acknowledging your pain is to repent to God.

2 Corinthians 7:10 (KJV) says, "**For godly sorrow worketh repentance to salvation** not to be repented of: but the sorrow of the world worketh death."

Repentance means to turn to God. You open the door to be delivered from sorrow when you turn to God. Turning to God includes acknowledging the sin that caused pain in your heart. Sin is anything that separates you from God. For example, one sin is not trusting God, by living a life without depending on God.

Pray the following prayer:

Lord,

Your word says in 1 John 1:9, that if I confess my sins that separated me from you and caused sorrow, you are faithful and just to forgive me and cleanse me from all unrighteousness. Lord, I confess my sin (confess the sin) _____. I receive your forgiveness. Thank you for cleansing me and removing sorrow from my heart.

In Jesus Name

Chapter 2

Life

"In him was life; and the life was the light of men."

John 1:4 (KJV)

I must admit, my definition of life was "doing." Life as I saw it was based on achieving goals and acquiring things. I felt I had to measure up to life by what I was achieving.

At the end of each year in my adult life, I evaluated my life by what I achieved. My goal-setting was getting the promotion, buying the home, getting the car, or buying the clothes. I focused on acquiring things by "doing."

This was the mindset I had when I became a certified speaker, trainer, and coach. My focus was on getting contracts with government, schools, or offering products. I was doing, doing, doing.... This mindset caused me to hit walls by not meeting my expectations. I recall how there was a void in my heart because I wasn't content with my achievements. I want you to reflect on your life for a moment by answering the following question:

Are you satisfied with your life?

Discontent is a sign that you are not living in the fullness of who you were created to be. I will show you later how having a mindset of "doing" creates discontent in your life.

What Is Life?

I shared my example of how I defined life and lived because life is about "being." Goals and planning are key to living desires in your heart, but they are only tools for you to achieve in life. Without you "being" who you were created to be, goals, planning, and achievements will leave a void in your heart. It's essential to know God's true definition of life.

Genesis 1:28 (KJV) says, "And God blessed them, and God said unto them, Be fruitful, and multiply, and replenish the earth, and subdue it: and have dominion over the fish of the sea, and over the fowl of the air, and over every living thing that moveth upon the earth."

God instructed mankind to "BE" fruitful, multiply, replenish, and have dominion. This call to action from God starts with you "being." God created you to be fruitful in talent, skills, and abilities. You were created to multiply with your influence. One definition of life is a state of being in force. Life is being who you are with beliefs, faith, action, momentum, strength, power, and vitality. God is love. God created you "to be" in his love defined in 1 Corinthians 13. Your "state of being" should include being patient, kind, trustworthy, protecting, hopeful, and persistent. This love doesn't fail. You are not a failure in God's love.

You Were Created To "Be"

When God looks at you, he sees strength, energy, power and momentum to act on the desires in your heart. Why? He sees himself connected to whom he created you to be, which identifies your state of being. Colossians 1:15 (NIV) says, "The Son is the image of the invisible God, the firstborn over all creation." Jesus is the image of God. He sacrificed his life so that you'd have the freedom to be who you were created to be in his image.

Jesus is your source of "being." This is why Jesus said in John 14:6 (KJV), "I am the way, the truth, and the life: no man cometh unto the Father, but by me." Jesus was confirming that he is literally the source of your life. This includes giving you the energy to be the force of your being.

The life that is in Jesus is the light (energy) for you to produce the desires from your heart. John 1:4 (KJV) says, "In him was life; and the life was the light of men." Jesus is your light (energy) for your "state of being." This means you have everything you need to discover and live the desires of your heart. Picture the core of an apple; there are seeds within that core that come from the apple. You enjoy the flesh of the apple but only experience the benefits of what the apple offers due to its core. Your authentic nature reflects the core of who you are in Jesus.

Your core includes the following:

- Unlimited Potential: Potential to live at your highest ability
- Strengths: Power of your mind; which is an intellectual force
- Complete: No defects in your authentic nature
- Sufficient: Qualified; competent to produce with character and productivity

Jesus had one rule to keep you in motion to live from your core. Jesus said in John 15:5 (NIV), "I am the vine; you are the branches. If you remain in me and I in you, you will bear much fruit; apart from me, you can do nothing." Jesus acknowledged you cannot live from your core without him.

George Washington Carver lived from his core. Carver, a devout Christian, described his moment of salvation when he was ten years old. He said, "God just came into my heart one afternoon while I was alone in the 'loft' of our big barn while I was shelling corn to carry to the mill to be ground into meal." George Washington lived from his core, the power of his mind, his intellect. Dr. Carver's approach to science was from his faith in God. He believed faith and science were connected to finding the truth about nature. Carver received an idea from God to instruct local farmers to plant peanuts. The popular seeds to plant were cotton. God gave Carver the intelligence to go against cultural norms. Booker T. Washington, President of Tuskegee, didn't agree with Carver's decision. George Washington Carver was not worried.

He said to Booker T Washington, "All my life, I have risen regularly at four in the morning to go into the woods and talk with God. That's where He reveals His secrets to me. When everybody else is asleep, I hear God best and learn my plan ... This morning, I asked Him why He made the peanut." Washington laughed at Carver's suggestion. He questioned Carver's decision and asked if God always gave him the right answers. Carver replied, "Let me put it this way: The Lord always provides me with life-changing ideas. Not that I am special. The Lord provides everyone with life-changing ideas. These ideas are quite literally a treasure from the Almighty. It is up to each of us; however, to choose and dig for the treasure." Within ten days, George Washington Carver had "discovered" more than 300 products from the peanut.

As a believer in Jesus since I was a child, I didn't live from my core. I received the gift of salvation. I didn't consult with Jesus about my life mission/purpose. I assumed life purpose was a personal preference. I believed God provided a buffet of options for your life purpose. I'm existing while I am centering my life on this belief that I have options to pursue desires in my heart. I considered Jesus when I had a need or a want. My faith was on standby when I exhausted all possibilities. God was my last option in planning my life. Here is the truth to what was happening to me. I lived separately from Jesus. I was not advancing in life.

In John 15:6 (KJV), Jesus said, "If a man abide not in me, he is cast forth as a branch, **and is withered**; and men gather them, and cast them into the fire, and they are burned." The definition of 'wither' is to fade; lose natural freshness; to become sapless. Your "state of being" begins to fade when you disconnect from Jesus. You lose a fresh perspective about life while your motivation and strength diminish. You live a life of existing. Exist means to live under adverse conditions. You live in a cycle of issues that work against you. For example, I lived in a cycle of people's opinion. I would make a decision based on a person's opinion. This worked against me and caused me not to pursue a business venture God desired for me to seek.

In 2004, God gave me a desire to buy into a franchise with an employment agency. For two weeks, I researched employment agencies. I took notes of agencies that offered a franchise. I built momentum to pursue this idea. I knew it was from God.

One day, I shared my idea with a person. I'm excited at the same time waiting for their opinion. My expectation of their opinion stopped my pursuit of opening an employment agency. This person immediately gave me reasons why I should not pursue this desire. I agreed with their view more than God's plans for my life. This is one way of disconnecting from Jesus. The desires hidden in your heart are connected to your identity in Christ. This includes abiding in Jesus. I was not living from the core of my identity in Christ.

"Be" Fruitful

Jesus approves of who you are in him. Why? He chose and appointed you to live from the core of who you are in him. In John 15:16 (NIV), Jesus said, "You did not choose me, but I chose you and appointed you so that you might go and bear fruit—fruit that will last—and so that whatever you ask in my name, the Father will give you."

Your success connects to the results Jesus chose and appointed you to produce. What works did Jesus appointed you to do? Jesus chose and appointed you to produce the desires of your heart, which is the following:

- Being who you were created to be in Jesus (Genesis 1:27)
- Living God's plans for your life (Jeremiah 29:11)

The foundation of living the desire of your heart produces the results of what Jesus called you to do. It's important to know your foundation of who you are in Jesus. Stay with me. We are still discussing the truth to life - your "state of being."

I mentioned how I allowed people's opinions to be the determining factor in the decisions I made. What do you immediately do when you get an idea? Do you look at your circumstances and determine if you should pursue the idea or not? The work Jesus chose you for may come in the form of an idea. An idea from God connects to the foundation of who you are. God looks at your heart to determine if you are advancing in "being" who you are in Christ. He examines whether your success is a result of what Jesus called you to do. The fruits Jesus chose and appointed you to produce are results of you advancing your life in Christ. Life advancement occurs when your spirit, soul, and body are abiding in Jesus. God fills the void in your heart as your life advances.

What is Life Advancement?

Think of the truth that Jesus chose and appointed you to produce fruit. You may not know what Jesus chose you to do. I guarantee you know where you are at in life. Now, think of where you want to be. There is a gap between where you are and where you want to be. Where you want to be is to produce the fruit Jesus chose and appointed you to produce. How do you close the gap? You close the gap through life advancement. Life advancement is accelerated growth. Your life advances when you:

1. Have a relationship with God: By knowing God's thoughts and ways

2. Be who you were created to be in Jesus: Your identity in Christ

3. Know how you were created: To have dominion over your life

4. Know the reason you were created: To love and serve people

By spiritual law, you are to grow from the foundation of who you are. Spiritual maturity occurs through spiritual growth. You advance your mind, will, and emotions when you grow spiritually.

Jesus desired to be a gift to the world by giving his life. At the age of twelve, Jesus' parents found him in the temple. Luke 2:46 (NIV) says, "After three days, they found him in the temple courts, sitting among the teachers, listening to them and asking them questions." Jesus set aside his divine nature and lived on earth in human nature. Jesus had to follow the law of human nature to sacrifice his life. Jesus had to grow in wisdom to advance in fulfilling his mission.

After Jesus left the temple, Luke 2:52 says, "And Jesus grew in wisdom and stature, and in favor with God and man." Jesus put into practice what he learned in the temple to grow in wisdom. Jesus lived a spiritual lifestyle to fulfill his life mission, and this is the same for you. To discover and live desires hidden in your heart, you must grow in wisdom. You speed up your growth when exercising God's teaching.

The Psychology of Life

I shared in the introduction that Jesus set you free to live the desires of your heart. In this chapter, I mentioned Jesus gives light (energy) for you to have power, strength, and momentum. This light is the freedom to live desires in your heart. You may ask, why are you not experiencing your desires since Jesus set you free? The answer: You have the responsibility to get God's knowledge to advance in your mind, will, and emotions. You enter the process of facing issues that work against you when you discover the desires in your heart. You will need your mind, will, and emotions to move past anything that works against you.

Here are some examples of life issues that work against you:

1. **Life circumstances** - circumstances that cause affliction, pain, distress, etc.

2. **Offense** – holding a grudge or resentment towards people or systems.

3. **Cares about life** – excessive concerns for yourself, people, and life. This includes worry, anxiety and over-analyzing issues.

4. **Living in the past** - not letting go of past disappointments by holding on to negative emotions of the past. The opposite is discussing past success to relive the feeling of success.

5. **Looking for others to approve you** - living life based on what others say about you. This turns into a life of people-pleasing. You deny yourself the truth of living your purpose.

6. **Getting wealth with deceit** – intentionally gain wealth through fraud and oppression towards people.

7. **Pursuing desires with wrong motives** – use manipulation or control for selfish gain.

8. **Looking for what society has to offer** - living your life based on cultural trends and what culture says is normal.

9. **Living with distractions** - allowing distractions to disrupt your daily life. This causes you to lose focus and drift through life.

You become discouraged when you deal with any of these factors for an extended time. Discouragement is strengthened in negative emotions. Discouragement is the enemy of your soul.

The following are roots to discouragement:

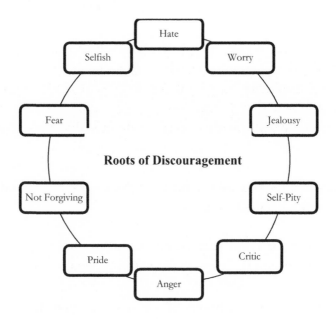

Roots of Discouragement

Hate

Worry

Selfish

Jealousy

Fear

Not Forgiving

Self-Pity

Pride

Critic

Anger

Discouragement will keep you from experiencing desires hidden in your heart. How do you move past discouragement? You must grow through the psychology of life.

Psychology is the doctrine of the soul. Life issues have a psychological effect on your soul (mind, will, and emotions). Your state of being is affected by issues. Jesus dealt with the psychological effects of your state of being when he was on the cross. In Isaiah 53, the verses describe Jesus' experience on the cross. He experienced rejection with many sorrows while he was acquainted with grief. This was Jesus' strategy for your well-being. Jesus didn't speak when he was on the cross. He continued to suffer mental anguish, negative emotions, affliction, oppression, etc.

Why didn't Jesus speak? He was thinking of you while pleasing God. Jesus knew you would lose out on life if he violated the spiritual law of sacrifice. He had to follow through with his death, burial, and resurrection. Jesus used knowledge to deal with the psychological effects of your soul.

Isaiah 53:11(KJV) says, "He shall see of the travail of his soul, and shall be satisfied: by his knowledge shall my righteous servant justify many; for he shall bear their iniquities." Jesus's knowledge of spiritual laws vindicated you to be free from the psychological effects of life factors you experienced.

You must have the knowledge of spiritual laws to grow through the psychology of life. God restores your soul (mind, will, and emotions) when you exercise spiritual laws. Psalm 19:7 (KJV) says, **"The law of the LORD is perfect, converting the soul**: the testimony of the LORD is sure, making wise the simple."** God's spiritual laws are the doctrine of psychology that restores your soul. Spiritual laws are the solution to mastering the psychology of life. The following are three truths to moving pass discouragement to live the desires hidden in your heart:

1. Have an Open Mind

I was a guest speaker for a parent group. I began to talk about discouragement. I'm no fan of discussing issues that cause people sadness. I believe in building people up by inspiring them with knowledge to help them move forward. God is a God of light. The starting point to advancing your life is knowing where you are. God does not want anyone to live his or her life in darkness. He makes you aware of where you are in life when you are feeling sad, depressed, anxious, angry, etc.

So, as I'm talking to the parent group about discouragement, I notice a parent becomes combative with me. It started out with her body posture and face expressing anger. Then came the attacks. She went on a 2-minute rant about her child. She was defensive about being in the parent group. The parent group was mandatory. I politely listened and addressed her concerns. After expressing her frustration, she abruptly left the room crying. I'm wondering as I'm speaking, what is agitating her? I knew her defense was not towards me.

Several parents stayed after the group session. They shared the awareness of what they learned from the session. A gentleman who was with the woman waited in line to speak to me. It was her husband. He shared with me that his wife wanted him to apologize on her behalf for leaving the room. He explained that as I was speaking, some issue from her childhood came up, and she could no longer sit with the group. My heart went out to her. I was sharing solutions to what she was dealing with. She could not go through the session. Why? Her mind was not open to receive knowledge to move forward in life. Her discouragement about life was stronger than her choice to get knowledge. Her mind remained closed to moving forward.

An open mind is needed to know where you are at and where you need to be. An open mind about God's word will help you overcome issues. You may not understand God's word, but an open mind will expand your understanding of his word. The key to having an open mind is receiving God's word as your truth. God's word will meet you where you are at and put you on the path that he has for you. Psalm 119:105 (KJV) says, "Thy word is a lamp unto my feet, and a light unto my path." This path is for you to experience the desires of your heart.

2. See Yourself – The Way God Sees You

Life has a way of affecting how you see yourself. You may have experienced a childhood that did not nurture who you were created to be. Some people may have ignored your unique personality and talents. You may have been teased, bullied, or assaulted for being you. I remember a time I was teased for liking to wear athletic attire. As a teenager, I preferred K-Swiss, and there was a friend who would tease my styling preference. This caused me to care more about how people viewed my style versus me "being" me. This caused me to see myself separate from my personal preference. I would settle for average or less in life because of how I viewed myself. God saw me in his image with talents and influenced my entire life. This is the same for you.

You must see yourself the way God sees you. Moving forward in life is based on your perspective. Perspective is your mental view of how you see yourself and your future. We live in a society where people are judged based on optics. People will measure you by your clothes, weight, gender, or skin color. They will ignore who you are in God's image. This may cause you to think that you must fix your outer appearance before you experience a change in your life. How you look is important, but God looks at the heart.

The desires in your heart are connected to you having the same view as God when you are nurturing desires. Your vision will be bigger than your budget during the season of nurturing your desire. You will be learning how to move past discouragement and life issues that have been holding you back.

I recall being discouraged when my professional head shot did not turn out the way I had expected. I had to believe God to get a professional one. I had favor with the photographer for a free session and three prints. I did not have a budget for a stylist nor a make-up artist. What caused me to keep moving forward? My perspective is what mattered as I was watering my desire, while God was looking at my heart. God was examining my growth and actions as well. God's view of you is based on who he created you to be and what you have hidden in your heart. It's important to have the same perspective as God.

3. Have Courage

Having courage is part of living desires of the heart. The key to overcoming issues is having the courage to discover desires hidden in your heart. The following is a story a gracious woman shared with me that is funny but full of wisdom:

"A man was walking down the street and saw an old man and his dog sitting on a porch. The dog was moaning while sitting on the porch. The man walked up to the porch and asked the old man why his dog was moaning. The old man said his dog was sitting on a nail. The man asked the old man, 'why doesn't your dog get off the nail.' The old man said, 'The nail doesn't hurt him enough."

Are you sitting on a "nail?" You may feel like you have no strength nor desire and feel comfortable staying where you are in life. Having courage is the solution to get off the "nail." The Latin word for courage is the heart. God will strengthen your heart when you dare to discover your heart desires. This includes the courage to grow spiritually. Psalm 31:24 (KJV) says, "Be of good courage, and he shall strengthen your heart, all ye that hope in the Lord." It's God's responsibility to strengthen your heart. Your job is to have courage with faith to depend on him. This starts with trusting him to move forward with your life. That takes courage. I had to deal with how I made myself my god, which caused me to get into depression. God began showing me how I used my heart to control my life, which produced anxiety. I had to learn how to trust God again. I had to be bold to do what God instructed me to do. How did I move forward? God was strengthening me to deal with depression while I was coordinating the mentoring group. I was working for the state government at the time. Clearly, church and state are not to be mixed with government affairs.

I was met with opposition from the manager. I received negative criticism from her. I needed the courage to move forward. My act of courage helped me pass the test God gave me to start the mentoring group. This put me on the path to discover more desires in my heart. I began to find my life in Jesus and plans God had for me. I would be stuck if I didn't dare to start the mentoring group. I would be in the cycle of dread, frustration, depression, and anxiety if I didn't have courage. The desires in your heart will take you out of your comfort zone. God will not give you the big picture. He will test you in steps. Your courage is needed to receive whom you are in Jesus and God's plans for your life. This is the life Jesus chose and appointed you to produce from your heart. This life includes the courage to live the desires of your heart.

Chapter 2 Summary

- Life is about "being," not "doing."
- Goals and planning are tools to make achievements in life.
- Life is "being" who you were created to be in God's image
- Life is God's call to action for you to be fruitful, multiply, replenish, and have dominion
- Jesus is your source to be who you were created to be in God's image. Jesus is the image of God. Colossians 1:15 (NIV) says, "The Son is the image of the invisible God, the firstborn over all creation."
- Jesus chose and appointed to remain in him
- You advance your life in Christ through spiritual growth
- You grow through the psychology of life by putting to practice God's Word
- **Move forward with:**
  1. An Open Mind
  2. Seeing yourself - the way God sees you
  3. Courage

A Call To Action

Sacrifice is giving up something, to experience something more significant. Jesus sacrificed his life so that you may live a life of significance. Desires of the heart come with your sacrifice to God.

What will you sacrifice to God to experience the desires in your heart?

God left a strategy for you to give a sacrifice to him. The sacrifice God desires from you is your heart. God wants the broken, discouraged heart you are holding on to. You may say, "it's too painful. My spirit is broken." Psalm 51:17 (KJV) says, **"The sacrifices of God are a broken spirit: a broken and a contrite heart, O God, thou wilt not despise."** A contrite heart is a heart full of regrets. God wants it all.

Pray the following prayer:

Lord,

I give you my broken spirit and discouraged heart in exchange for a whole spirit and courageous heart. I give you my weakness, for your strength; my flawed nature, for your divine nature. I give you depression and anxiety for dependence on you; failures, for success. I give anger, for your calmness; negativity, for your positivity; regrets, for satisfaction with you. I give you the past, for a future with you; toxic relationships, for a relationship with you; pain, for your joy; defeat, for your victory. I give you me, to be all who you created me to be in Jesus. Thank you for receiving my spirit and heart as my sacrifice to you.

In Jesus Name.

Meditate

Take at least five minutes with no distractions and meditate on Psalm 51.

Chapter 3

Rest

"Therefore, since the promise of entering his rest still stands,
let us be careful that none of you be found
to have fallen short of it."

Hebrews 4:1 (NIV)

Rest is your first action step to discovering and living the desires in your heart. **You must REST in God!** Resting in God is a requirement to experience desires in your heart. This means to stop thinking and living life your way. Resting is connected to your commitment to seek God with your whole desire. Only God can give you rest when you commit to seeking him. 2 Chronicles 15:15 confirms that rest from God comes when you commit to seeking God with your full desire and whole heart. The scripture says, "And all Judah rejoiced at the oath: for they had sworn with all their heart, and sought him with their whole desire; and he was found of them: and the LORD gave them rest round about." (2 Chronicles 15:15 KJV)

Resting is a call to action from Jesus. Here is Jesus message to You: **"Are you tired? Worn out? Burned out on religion? Come to me.** Get away with me, and you'll recover your life. I'll show you how to take a real rest. Walk with me and work with me—watch how I do it. Learn the unforced rhythms of grace. I won't lay anything heavy or ill-fitting on you. Keep company with me, and you'll learn to live freely and lightly." Matthew 11:28-30 (MSG)

You must run to Jesus, no matter what you are going through. Only Jesus has the knowledge and power for you to move past life circumstances that block you from experiencing the desires in your heart. I remember how the depression I was experiencing was so painful that words could not describe the pain that was in my heart. I was at the breaking point of death. Desire, motivation, joy, confidence, and peace was sapped out of me. I knew if I didn't confront the issue, I was going to regress rapidly in life.

I thank God that there was one thing that was not sapped out of me, and that was my **BELIEF in God**. Including the **BELIEF that only God could fix my life**. I'm grateful that I had the sense to run to **HIM**. I recall sitting in a rocking chair, just crying in pain. The Lord softly spoke to me, "Get in your purpose."

I wanted God to fix things that were out of control in my life before living my purpose. What was God's reason to instruct me to get in my purpose? He was instructing me to rest. Are you waiting on God to change a situation in your life? You may be thinking to yourself, "I have been praying to God. I am still dealing with the same cycle of life issues." The life issues may be suffocating you. You want God to answer your prayer, so you can breathe. You may be tired. Tired to the point that you have no energy to do anything. There are four C's that will keep you dealing with the same life issues:

1. **Complacent:** This involves being satisfied with certain areas of your life that block desires in your heart. Complacency kills dreams.

2. **Comfort Zone:** This involves staying connected to people, environments, tasks, or commitments you have outgrown. Comfort zones stunt your growth and potential.

3. **Compromise:** Commitments that jeopardize the truth of who you are, your values, morals, influence, etc. Compromise causes you to settle for average. This

creates a mindset of being indifferent about specific areas of your life.

4. **Complain:** Consistently expressing resentment with murmurs and fault-finding. Complaining expresses bitterness and pain in your mind without gratitude towards God.

It's important to identify if you are in any of the four areas regarding your life. The four C's cancels out God granting you desires in your heart. Proverbs 10:24 (KJV) says, "The fear of the wicked, it shall come upon him: but the desire of the righteous shall be granted." Desires in the heart are the cure for complacency, comfort zone, compromise, and complaining. God will test you to see if you are holding in your heart anything that is allowing you to be in a comfort zone, complacent, compromising, or complaining place in life.

God's answers prayers for those whose desires are influenced by his grace. God recognizes you are thirsty through your desires when you put into action what he instructed you to do. Isiah 55:1 (MSG) says, **"Hey there! All who are thirsty, come to the water!"** Your thirst represents your need for God to be your source to live. Water in this scripture means your source to life. You must rest in God now that you recognize the answer to your thirst. It's natural to think of rest as a place where you can go to a beach and enjoy the water and sun. Or a day of just doing nothing. You have an idea of what this type of rest means to you. Resting in God is spiritual. It's not the rest you naturally think about.

What is Rest?

Spiritual rest in Christ is taking your rightful position with God. This includes receiving God's covenant when you received the gift of salvation from Jesus. One formal definition for rest is to cease from action. I was agitated in my mind profoundly with depression to the point I could not have a productive day.

God instructed me to focus on him for 30 days by meditating on certain scriptures. The first two weeks were challenging because there was a battle in my mind between receiving God's word and issues that took up residence in my mind. You know how you can rehearse problems over and over in your mind to the point you will talk about it to anyone who will listen. The issue greets you in the morning. You give attention to it while you are starting your day. You may call someone to discuss it. You drive to work and listen to music that may reinforce what you are going through. You connect with the person at work to talk about it again. You ask someone to go to lunch with you to discuss it.

Or you may be the person who keeps busy. You wake up. You start cleaning. You're consumed with the issue in your heart, but you are handling tasks. People come to you because you get the job done, but they don't know that your excessive productivity is a band-aid to cover the pain you have in your heart. Whatever your method is to cope with life issues, the fact remains that there is a pain in your heart that is weighing you down, and negative emotions are the songs of the day. This is the battle that wars in your mind when you begin to rest in God. You experience the following when you take your rightful position to rest in God:

- Your spirit, soul and body become quiet
- You trust God
- You receive more of God's instructions and guidance
- Life problems no longer disturb you
- Your mind is calm without anxiety
- You focus on God's promises for your life
- Your decisions are based on God's truth

- God defends you with his truth

At the end of my 30-day journey, my mind was quiet. I could hear God's voice more than the sound of my circumstances. I was resting in God. My conditions did not change. I didn't know the desires in my heart, but I was taking the position to receive from God. I was reconciling my life with God. To find rest in God, you must stop thinking of your way by renewing your mind to God's word. Resting in God is connected to a spiritual lifestyle in Christ. How you live your life spiritually in Christ is the determining factor in experiencing desires in your heart. Mental rest comes from God. Only God can give rest through Christ. This is why Jesus said come to me and I will give you rest. **Rest includes the following:**

1. Believing God

Do you believe God? Resting is connected to you believing God. I will start with the basic level of your faith. What was the first requirement for you to become a Christian? It was you believing in your heart that God raised Jesus from the dead while you made the confession that Jesus is Lord. Romans 10:9 (NIV) says, "If you declare with your mouth, 'Jesus is Lord,' and believe in your heart that God raised him from the dead, you will be saved." Your salvation in Jesus is based on your belief. Now, we will go further. Are you experiencing desires in your heart in every area of life? This is where you have to identify on a deeper level of your belief in God. Do you believe God can produce desires in your heart? Do you believe God will produce desires in your heart when you are facing the impossible in your life?

God promised the children of Israel a land full of resources. The children of Israel were to believe God for their promise while they were in the wilderness. Moses sent 12 spies to confirm if the land of Canaan were full of resources which God promised to the children of Israel. Only 2 out of 12 spies acknowledged they could take possession of the land. The ten spies saw themselves as not capable of taking possession of the land God promised them. The children of Israel who didn't believe God started a campaign of complaining by discussing how they could come up with a better way to end their suffering in the wilderness. God was displeased. Numbers 14:11 (NIV) says, "The LORD said to Moses, 'How long will these people treat me with contempt?

How long will they refuse to believe in me, in spite of all the signs I have performed among them?"

The children of Israel's hearts were detached from God delivering them from slavery. Their minds were agitated by their experience in the wilderness, which caused them to get in a state of unrest, separate from God. Belief is resting in God. The children of Israel could not enter into the rest of God because of their unbelief. Hebrews 3:18-19 (NIV) says, "And to whom did God swear that they would never enter his rest if not to those who disobeyed? [19] So we see that they were not able to enter, because of their unbelief." God just wanted the children of Israel to believe him. God didn't let them enter the promised land because of their unbelief.

Here, the catch to resting in God to live desires in your heart, you must be ALL IN with your belief in God. This means, if you are 65 years old and never been married, you must believe God to bless you with a God-fearing spouse. You must believe God to open a school. You must believe God will give you a new career at the age of 55. You must believe God will give you a profitable business after failing in many business attempts. You must believe God will restore your life. This is all based on what you believe. Your belief is necessary because Jesus paid the price for you to experience desires hidden in your heart. Jesus paid the price for you to have divine health, financial wealth, loving relationships, a peaceful spirit, positive emotions, a sound mind, etc.

2. Receiving Jesus as Your Great High Priest

Jesus paid the price to become the great high priest of your covenant with God. By spiritual law, no person can go to God regarding life matters without a high priest. A high priest was appointed to represent people of God under the Old Covenant. God instructed Jesus to come into the earth to be the great high priest over your life under the New Covenant. Therefore, resting in God includes you receiving Jesus as your great high priest. Jesus understands you and the life challenges you experience. This means Jesus feels your loneliness, rejection, pain, insecurities, disappointments, etc.

Hebrews 4:15 (NIV) says, "For we do not have a high priest who is unable to empathize with our weaknesses, but we have one who has been tempted in every way, just as we are—yet he did not sin." Unresolved issues in your heart begin to come out when you enter the process of discovering the desires in your heart. I didn't realize how I changed the way I dressed because of what was said to me. From my mid-twenties thru early thirties, I took pride in how I dressed. I felt in my heart that dressing nicely was part of displaying who I am.

One day, a person of influence made a statement that single women are dressing up just to get a man's attention. I absorbed this belief. I stopped dressing with pride so men wouldn't think I was attempting to get their attention. This may seem small or insignificant, but this clogged my heart. God created me to dress with pride. It is not based on getting attention. This is based on the truth that God fearfully and wonderfully made me. This was a barrier that scarred my self-image. God will reveal to you what scarred your self-image. Those scars will cause you to think you are unworthy of experiencing the desires placed in your heart.

Jesus is your high priest that validates your identity and removes scars so you can live in the freedom of who you are with confidence. This is connected to the truth that Jesus is the way, the truth, and the life, confirmed in John 14:6.

This is having confidence in who you were created to be. What issues from your past pops up in your mind?

What issues stir negative emotions when you reflect on your life? Whatever issues you are facing now or in the future, Jesus is available to help you in the time of need. Receiving Jesus as your high priest is holding on to your faith by acknowledging him during challenging times. Hebrews 4:14 (NIV) says, **"Therefore, since we have a great high priest who has ascended into heaven, Jesus the Son of God, let us hold firmly to the faith we profess."** You must hold tight to your faith and receive Jesus as your high priest, knowing he will take care of issues that try to stop you from experiencing the desires in your heart. So, rest by receiving Jesus as your great high priest.

3. Agreeing with God in Your Mind

When you accepted Jesus as your Lord and Savior in your heart, you entered into a covenant with God. Resting includes playing your part in your covenant with God. God's covenant with you is an in-depth study of its own. One definition of God's covenant is the agreement of minds. Your covenant with God includes promises that are connected to the desires of your heart. Therefore, you have a guaranteed yes from God for every promise attached to the desires in your heart. 2 Corinthians 1:20 (KJV) says, "For all the promises of God in him are yea, and in him Amen, unto the glory of God by us." Do you agree with God regarding his promises for your life?

Your agreement with God starts in your mind. The laws of God's covenant with you are placed in your mind. There are spiritual laws you must live by to rest in God. A spiritual law that is challenging to agree with God in your mind is loving your enemies -- people who repeatedly violated you. You may find them to be intentionally using you or defaming your character. The royal law of love is a spiritual law you must agree with God in your mind. James 2:8 (NIV) says, "If you really keep the royal law found in Scripture, 'Love your neighbor as yourself,' you are doing right." When you agree with this law, God will empower you to love your enemies. God was placing his spiritual laws in my mind when I was meditating on his word for 30 days. I was finding rest in God as I was agreeing with his word in my mind. Hebrews 8:10 (KJV) says, "This is the covenant I will establish with the people of Israel after that time, declares the Lord. I will put my laws in their minds and write them on their hearts. I will be their God, and they will be my people." Your agreement with God in your mind is resting in God.

4. Valuing God's Message to You

Do you give full attention to your Bible? God looks to see if you value his message in the Bible. The Bible is a message from God to you. 2 Timothy 3:16-17 (NIV) says, "All Scripture is God-breathed and is useful for teaching, rebuking, correcting and training in righteousness, so that the servant of God may be thoroughly equipped for every good work." God's message to you in the Bible does the following:

- Breathes life into your spirit, soul (mind, will, and emotions), and body
- Teaches you
- Disapproves of your wrong thoughts and actions
- Gives you a standard to live by
- Trains you on how to put into action God's truth
- Gives you the discipline to be consistent in your spiritual lifestyle
- Conforms your heart to God's truth

God's message through the Bible is to equip you to live a successful life. A successful life that is aligned with his thoughts and ways.

You receive God's rest when you value his message. You place value on God's word by accepting it over anything opposite of his truth. God has good news for you in the midst of additional information you consume daily. Every day, you are bombarded with information. We absorb information from television, email, social media, text message, phone notifications, etc. This information challenges the truth of God's word in your heart. The information you give the most attention to is the one you value. Once you receive information consistently, you begin to believe it is normal, especially if the information is in agreement with your current circumstances.

This causes fear to settle in your heart.

You receive this information as truth opposite of God's message to you. Your mind, will, and emotions get agitated (nervous, stressed, restless, etc.). Next, you become worried, depressed, and anxious. This is the opposite of resting in God. The children of Israel did not get rest in God because they did not value God's message. Hebrews 4:2 (NIV) says, "For we also have had the good news proclaimed to us, just as they did; but the message they heard was of no value to them, because they did not share the faith of those who obeyed." Without rest, the children of Israel could not enter into the promised land. The great news for you is, when you value God's message, you get the rest you need. Your rest puts you in the position to discover and live the desires in your heart.

5. Engaging Your Life with God's Knowledge

God's knowledge is key to resting in God. Think of a time when your back was against the wall in any particular situation. Your response would be, if it had not been for God who was on my side, your back would remain against the wall. I know in your trouble you received God's knowledge to get you out of your dilemma. You prayed, and God gave you the knowledge to escape. You have God's wisdom recorded in your testimony.

Do you depend on God's knowledge for every area in your life? Your mind was created to receives God's knowledge.

During the process of discovering the desires in my heart, God told me that I would have to think my way through this process. God's knowledge will help you engage your life as a strategic thinker.

Jesus engaged his life in God's knowledge. Jesus needed God's knowledge to instruct the disciples, heal the sick, and raise the dead. Jesus employed God's knowledge for his death, burial, and resurrection. He made it a priority to use his time and energy to get God's knowledge for his life.

Jesus was 12 years old when his family went to Jerusalem for the feast of Passover. He went to a temple instead of returning home with his family. When Jesus family found him in the temple, Mary asked, "Why have you treated us like this?" Mary worried about Jesus and wondered why he left them. Jesus response to Mary is found in Luke 2:49 (KJV), which says, "And he said unto them, How is it that ye sought me? wist ye not that I must be about my Father's business?" Jesus engaged his life by making God's business his number priority. Jesus was getting God's knowledge in the temple. You must engage your life by making God's business your number one priority. This happens when you engage your life with God's knowledge. Reading this book is one example of you engaging your life by getting God's knowledge.

God's spirit rests on you when you engage your life to get his knowledge. Isaiah 11:2 (KJV) says, "And the spirit of the LORD shall rest upon him, the spirit of wisdom and understanding, the spirit of counsel and might, the spirit of knowledge and of the fear of the LORD." This scripture is referencing Jesus. God's spirit rested upon Jesus while he lived God's plans for his life. Jesus is the image of God. You were created in God's image. God spirit will rest upon you when you get God's knowledge.

I began to fully engaged my life when I joined the John Maxwell Team. I laugh as I tell you, but I joined to learn how to set up my business to serve professional athletes. I went to the International Maxwell Certification assuming I was going to learn how to write contracts to get professional athletes service. I was way off with my assumption.

My first day at the conference was my divine appointment with God. God expanded my awareness of who I was in him. Most importantly, I entered the process on learning how to engage my life with God's knowledge. I knew then God was putting me on the path to know how I was created as I learned methods of personal growth. During this process, I was discovering how I was created through the lens of science. I was getting God's knowledge on the laws of human nature, universal laws, life principals, and spiritual laws. God's spirit rested upon me to know Jesus in my mind, will, and emotions. I prospered in my soul when I engaged my life with God's knowledge. I didn't fully understand the importance of thriving in my mind, will, and emotions until I discovered how to engage my life with Jesus' teachings.

Most of my life, I went to church every Sunday but expected God's promises without putting into action God's instructions. Your responsibility as a follower of Christ is to engage your life through discipleship. The meaning of disciple is to learn. Discovering and living desires from your heart are connected to your discipleship in Christ. You must ask yourself: Have I answered the call of discipleship from Jesus? The only way you will know is if you engaged your life in God's knowledge. This is where you find rest in God.

Chapter 3 Summary:

- Resting in God is a requirement to experience desires in your heart.
- **There are four C's that will keep you dealing with the same life issues:**
  1. **Complacent:** This involves being satisfied with certain areas of your life that block desires in your heart. Complacency kills dreams.
  2. **Comfort Zone:** This involves staying connected to people, environments, tasks, or commitments you have outgrown. Comfort zones stunt your growth and potential.
  3. **Compromise:** Commitments that jeopardize the truth of who you are, your values, morals, influence, etc. Compromise causes you to settle for average. This creates a mindset of being indifferent about specific areas of your life.
  4. **Complain:** Consistently expressing resentment with murmurs and fault-finding. Complaining expresses bitterness and pain in your mind without gratitude towards God.
- Resting is connected to your commitment to seek God will all your heart.

- Resting in God is receiving God's covenant
- Resting in God is to stop doing things your way
- **Resting includes:**
  1. Believing God
  2. Receiving Jesus as your high priest
  3. Agreeing with God in your mind
  4. Valuing God's message to you
  5. Engaging your life with God's knowledge

A Call To Action

Stop doing things your way! This is the strategic way to take action on resting in God. Beliefs drive behavior. Your belief in God is what will drive your behavior to act on the desires of your heart.

What is bothering you?

I challenge you to stop thinking about it for 30 days. You are telling God you believe he will deliver you from the situation when you make the decision to stop thinking about what is bothering you. Isaiah 54:14 (KJV) says, "In righteousness shalt thou be established: thou shalt be far from oppression; for thou shalt not fear: and from terror; for it shall not come near thee." Oppression, fear, nor terror has no power over you when you are in right standing with God. God will give you rest from your enemies the same way he gave Solomon rest from his enemies. 1 Chronicles 22:9 (KJV) says, "Behold, a son shall be born to thee, who shall be a man of rest; and I will give him rest from all his enemies round about: for his name shall be Solomon, and I will give peace and quietness unto Israel in his days." Receive God's rest for your life!

Pray the following prayer,

Lord,

I make the decision now to stop thinking about _____ (tell God what is bothering you). I believe you will give me rest from this situation because I am in right standing with you. I give you my cares and worry about this situation. I receive by faith your instruction and guidance to move past this circumstance with your freedom, peace, confidence. I affirm your rest surrounds me. Thank you for giving me rest.

In Jesus Name.

Meditate

Read Hebrews Chapter 4 for 30 days. Meditate on this chapter in a quiet place without distractions.

Chapter 4

Trust God

"Trust in him at all times; ye people, pour out your heart before him: God is a refuge for us. Selah."

Psalm 62:8 (KJV)

Now that you made the decision to rest in the Lord, you will receive guidance that leads to the truth of who you are in Jesus. Including the pleasure in knowing God. The Holy Spirit will guide you into your truth. A guide will take you places you never experienced. I love the experience of a museum docent, a guide for museum visitors. Their purpose is to give visitors the best experience and knowledge of the museum. The docent has a strategy on how to lead you; they will provide you with knowledge about time periods, artifacts, paintings, etc. People allow museum docents to lead because they trust their guidance.

The Holy Spirit is your guide to discover the desires in your heart. This is why it's important to rest. You receive the Holy Spirit's guidance while resting in God. The Holy Spirit will guide you as you trust God.

Trusting God

Trusting God is making a commitment to allow God full access to your heart. Psalm 62:8 (KJV) says, "Trust in him at all times; ye people, pour out your heart before him: God is a refuge for us. Selah." Trust involves you letting go of dead issues that caused your heart pain or distress. God becomes your refuge when you let go of what concerns you. A refuge is a place of protection. You exchange your life issues for God's protection when you trust him. God is your refuge from negativity, doubts, insecurities, self-judgment, guilt, shame, etc. The strategy for trusting God is to renew your mind. Romans 12:2 (KJV) says, "And be not conformed to this world: **but be ye transformed by the renewing of your mind,** that ye may prove what is that good, and acceptable, and perfect will of God." You are able to identify desires when you renew your mind in God's word. Your mind reveals your intentions, will, and desire. Psalms 40:8 (NIV) says, "**I desire to do your will, my God; your law is within my heart.**" How does God know that you want to live his will? God looks at your heart and tests your mind to see if you are desiring his will for your life. Jeremiah 17:10 (NIV) says, **"I the LORD search the heart and examine the mind, to reward each person according to their conduct, according to what their deeds deserve."** This is God's way of determining if you are trusting him.

Renewing your mind to God's word builds you up spiritually and mentally. Edification occurs when you trust God in renewing your mind to his word. The Webster Dictionary 1828 Edition defines edification as the improvement and progress of the mind, in knowledge, in morals, in faith, and holiness. Your mind advances in God's knowledge through edification. Edifying your mind in God's knowledge protects your life from being destroyed. Hosea 4:6 (KJV) says, "My people are destroyed for lack of knowledge: because thou hast rejected knowledge, I will also reject thee, that thou shalt be no priest to me: seeing thou hast forgotten the law of thy God, I will also forget thy children."

The following are ways to identify if you are trusting God to edify your mind:

- You allow God to instruct you on how to live your life (Psalms 32:8)

- You receive God's word as your truth (John 17:17)

- You allow the Holy Spirit to guide you into all truth (John 16:13)

- You allow God's law in your mind through meditation (Joshua 1:8)

- You put God's knowledge into action in your daily living while discovering and experiencing the desires in your heart (James 1:22)

Where Are You?

Trusting God is allowing God's word to examine where you're at. You may have hidden in your mind guilt and shame from your past which is painful to deal with. Your mind is irritated, where you don't want to face your future. You hold in your mind silent frustration, dread, and discouragement. I want you to understand it is natural for you to feel this way. This is your conscious, which is your power of knowing where you're at in life.

Genesis 3:9 (NIV) says, **"But the LORD God called to the man, 'Where are you?"** God designed you to use your conscious to be aware of where you are at and where you need to be. Adam only associated with weakness, failure, and negative emotions when God asked, "Where are you?" Adam explained he hid because he was naked and afraid. I want you to stop reading for a moment to answer the following questions:

How do you feel when God is touching your heart to move forward?

How do you respond when you are taken out of your comfort zone?

What are your thoughts when God asks you to do something you have never done?

The answers to these questions make you aware of where you're at consciously. There is no right or wrong answer. However, there is a right and wrong way to respond. I want you to understand how trusting God to edify your mind plays a part in your conscious.

Your conscious is not for you to afflict yourself with negative emotions, shame, guilt, nor thoughts of unworthiness.

This causes you to isolate yourself from experiencing the truth of who you are in Jesus. God expects for you to use your conscious to connect with his truth. The right way to respond is by trusting the Holy Spirit to guide you into your truth. I had to face this awareness when I was dealing with anxiety and depression. It's natural to just cope with negative emotions. God did not create you to cope with anything that keeps you from experiencing the truth of who you are. Negative emotions are indicators that it's time to connect to the truth of who you are in Jesus Christ. The foundation of your desire is related to who you were created to be and to live God's plans for your life.

Psalm 119:105 (KJV) says, "Thy word is a lamp unto my feet, and a light unto my path." God's word shines light on you being aware of where you're at and where you need to be in Jesus Christ. In John 4, Jesus sat on Jacob's well and interacted with a Samaritan woman who came to draw water from the well. Jesus asked the woman for water to drink. I want to point out the woman's response to Jesus. John 4:9 (NIV) says, "The Samaritan woman said to him, 'You are a Jew, and I am a Samaritan woman. How can you ask me for a drink?' (For Jews do not associate with Samaritans.)" Jesus asked the woman to do something she never did before. Her response to Jesus was based on the logic of cultural expectations. During this time, Jews did not associate with Samaritans.

In John 4:10 (NIV), "Jesus answered her, 'If you knew the gift of God and who it is that asks you for a drink, you would have asked him, and he would have given you living water." In John 4:11 (NIV), "the woman said, 'you have nothing to draw with, and the well is deep. Where can you get this living water?" The Samaritan woman went from cultural expectations to thinking with limitations. Jesus knew of her status and limited thiking. Jesus wanted her to connect to the truth of who she was in him. He was offering her the opportunity to trust God to be her source for living.

This the same for you! God uses the desires in your heart for you to trust him to be your source for living. The communication between Jesus and the Samaritan continued until she received his truth in her heart. The Samaritan woman separated herself from cultural expectations, limited thinking, and her past, to receive Jesus. This is the same for you. God wants you to separate yourself from cultural expectations, your weaknesses and your history by trusting in him.

Are You "Woke"?

I use the term "woke" because it has become a popular term in our time. The term "woke" refers to being aware of issues concerning social and racial injustice. I believe it is our duties as Christians to be consciously aware of social and racial injustice. I wanted to use this term as an example of you being "woke" to the truth of who you are. If Jesus was sitting in front of you and asked, "Are you woke?" He would be referring to who you are in Him. Jesus would want to know if you used your conscious to be aware of who you are in Him. Ephesians 5:14 (KJV) says, "Wherefore he saith, Awake thou that sleepest, and arise from the dead, and Christ shall give thee light." Edification includes awakening to the truth that Jesus is the light to you living in God's image. You were made righteous to live in light of Jesus Christ. This is why your limitations, weakness, failures, etc. are not barriers to you experiencing the desires of your heart. I Corinthians 15:34 (KJV), "Awake to righteousness, and sin not; for some have not the knowledge of God: I speak this to your shame." You must believe this and hold this truth by faith. You discover desires in your heart when you are "woke" to your righteousness in Christ.

Your righteousness through Christ is added to you when you believe in God. Galatians 3:6 (KJV) says, "Even as Abraham believed God, and it was accounted to him for righteousness." This comes with trusting God with all of your heart.

Edification in Action

I've been a Christian since I was a child. I was awakened to my right standing with God through Jesus in my adult years. I was faithful in attending church on Sundays, including being committed to serving in the church. I would get excited about my new awareness of God's promises to me.

During the week, I would continue to pray and read my Bible. I knew how to pray to God to get my needs met, but I didn't depend on God when I was faced with my limitations, weaknesses and failures to live the desires in my heart. Hidden in my heart were dead issues from my past. I accepted life as it was. This caused me to become stuck. What happened? It was not God's fault.

I was not progressing my mind in Christ. I was "woke" but frustrated, depressed, anxious, angry, and dreading everything about life. I wasn't trusting God. Yet, I was holding onto God's promises in misery.

My story is an example of being "woke" consciously but unfulfilled. What changed? I needed to put God's knowledge into action. I was edified, but I didn't practice what I learned. There is a difference between conscious and conscience. Conscious is the awareness part of your mind. Conscience is the part of your mind that knows how to put God's truth into action. This is where you know God and Jesus. The Webster Dictionary 1828 Edition identifies conscience as the original faculty of human nature. The Latin word for conscience is to know. Your conscience is your internal self-knowledge or judgment of right or wrong to decide on your own emotions or actions. Your conscience strengthens when you act on God's word by faith. It's is the place where God's thoughts and ways operate. You are convicted by your conscience when you become aware of God's truth.

In John 8, The scribes and Pharisees brought a woman who committed adultery to Jesus. They wanted to know from Jesus how he would serve the woman consequences for her sin. Jesus told them that anyone with sin should cast the first stone. John 8:9 (KJV) says, "And they which heard it, **being convicted by their own conscience,** went out one by one, beginning at the eldest, even unto the last: and Jesus was left alone, and the woman standing in the midst." The scribes and Pharisees came into the knowledge of God's truth, which convicted them. Your conviction of God's word allows the knowledge of God's laws to enter your conscience.

During the process of edification, it's important to recognize your convictions when you become more aware of yourself. God's truth is like a mirror; it will show you things about yourself that you wouldn't usually recognize without a mirror. You can't adequately put on make-up or shave without a mirror. I would look like a clown if I put on make-up without looking in the mirror, but with the mirror, I make sure I'm looking my best.

Conviction allows you to look your best. It enables you to receive truth while self-judgment will allow you to reject the truth. While you are reading this book, you may feel guilty about something through self-judgment. Self-judgment may include not using your time wisely, not eating healthy, worrying about your future, not accomplishing a goal, etc. Self-judgment cancels out you experiencing God's will for your life. Hebrews 9:14 (KJV) says, "How much more shall the blood of Christ, who through the eternal Spirit offered himself without spot to God, purge your conscience from dead works to serve the living God?" Jesus paid the price with his blood to purge your conscience from actions that bring self-judgment. Convictions help you experience a conscience free of guilt, shame, and self-judgment.

Jesus is not with you in the physical to help you recognize the truth. He left you with the Holy Spirit. This is why Jesus instructed his disciples to wait for the Holy Spirit. Acts 2:4 (NIV) says, "All of them were filled with the Holy Spirit and began to speak in other tongues as the Spirit enabled them." I remember as a teenager sitting in a pew during a Bible study at New Jerusalem Full Gospel Baptist Church in Flint, MI. Bishop Odis Floyd was teaching on the Holy Spirit. I remember while he was teaching, saying, "Receive the Holy Spirit in your heart." I felt the Holy Spirit's presence in my heart while speaking in tongues as Bishop Floyd was teaching. Your conscience confirms the truth through the Holy Spirit. Romans 9:1 (NIV) says, "I speak the truth in Christ—I am not lying; my conscience confirms it through the Holy Spirit." You have the power to put God's truth into action with your conscience.

Move Forward

I remember a former co-worker would often say, "I can't think." Her work performance showed she was fully competent in performing job duties. It's when she was overwhelmed with the stressors from the job she couldn't think clearly. Your conscience gives you the ability to think when you edify your mind with God's knowledge. You can think pass your limitations, stressors, or any type of barrier that is opposite of your truth.

You experience a sound mind through your conscience. 2 Timothy 1:7 (KJV) says, **"For God hath not given us the spirit of fear; but of power, and of love, and of a sound mind."** Power, love, and a sound mind will empower you to experience the desires in your heart.

The following are four truths to trust God while edifying your mind in his truth:

1. Keep a Heart of Repentance

Sin is anything that separates your dependence on God. We have the opportunity daily to sin. There is no big sin or little sin. Whatever sin that is in your life, it cannot have dominion over you without your permission. Romans

6:14 (KJV) says, "For sin shall not have dominion over you: for ye are not under the law, but under grace." Be quick to repent when anything is separating you from God. Sin hinders you from progressing your mind in God's knowledge. 1 John 1:9 (KJV) says, "If we confess our sins, he is faithful and just to forgive us our sins, and to cleanse us from all unrighteousness." Stay in right standing with God to experience the desires in your heart.

2. Receive Power from the Holy Spirit

You were created to depend on God. God is fully aware that you cannot advance your life without Him. This is why Jesus gave his life to reconcile your life back to God. Most importantly to be the person you were created to be in Christ. Holy Spirit is God's promise for you to live the desires in your heart. This is why Jesus instructed his disciples to wait for the Holy Spirit. The disciples needed the power to advance God's plans for their life. This is the same for you. You need the power of the Holy Spirit to live God's plans for your life. In Acts 1:8 (NIV) Jesus said, **"But you will receive power when the Holy Spirit comes on you;"** Ask God to fill you with the Holy Spirit with evidence of speaking in tongue. Receive the Holy Spirit by faith. It's your faith that brings results from the spirit realm. Acts 2:4 (NIV) says, "All of them were filled with the Holy Spirit and began to speak in other tongues as the Spirit enabled them."

3. Pray in Tongues

Praying in tongues is the most misunderstood virtue. You pray the perfect will of God for your life when you pray in tongues. You are communicating with God in mysteries when praying in tongues. I Corinthians 14:2 (NIV) says, "**For anyone who speaks in a tongue does not speak to people but to God. Indeed, no one understands them; they utter mysteries by the Spirit."**

Praying in tongues progresses your mind (edify) to know how to deal with situations.

I Corinthians 14:4 (NIV) says, **"Anyone who speaks in a tongue edifies themselves, but the one who prophesies edifies the church."**

I can share many stories of how God showed me how to deal with situations when I prayed in tongues. One morning before my husband went to work, I felt negative emotions. I sat at the table and prayed in tongues. God instructed me to pray for my husband before he left for work. I asked God to give him a solution that he would need that day. My husband left for work. He called while he was commuting to inform me that he was returning home due to a tire "not sounding right." He took the car to the tire shop. They informed him that the tire was loose. If he kept driving to work, the tire would have rolled off the car. Speaking in tongues gives you the solution to move past situations or limitations. Jude 20 (NIV) says, "But you, dear friends, by building yourselves up in your most holy faith and praying in the Holy Spirit." You are praying in the Holy Spirit when you pray in tongues. I speak in tongues daily. This edifies me to keep my mind focused on how to put God's truth into action. Ask God for understanding if you need more knowledge about speaking in tongues.

4. Show Yourself Love

Edification includes loving God, yourself, and people. 1 Corinthians 8:1 (KJV) **says,** "Now about food sacrificed to idols: We know that We all possess knowledge." But knowledge puffs up while love builds up."

I want to focus on loving yourself in this chapter. I am convinced that people love God. I've witnessed people expressing their love towards God. They acknowledge with joy and gratitude for what God has done for them. Also, I observe the same people not showing love towards themselves. This is a red flag that they genuinely do not love who they are, flaws and all. Do you look in the mirror and tell yourself, "I love you?" I challenge you to do a quick exercise. Here are the instructions for the exercise:

1. Go to a mirror, look into your eyes with a smile.
2. Tell yourself with a smile, "I love you."
3. Take in the moment by reflecting on what happened.
4. Write down your experience

I challenged you to do the exercise because you are the one who knows the depth of your self-love. I guarantee that everyone will have different experiences. This exercise is an example of edifying yourself. The truth to loving on yourself brings you into awareness of who you are. You get the strength to see yourself the way God created you. Your mind makes a connection with your hidden potential. Showing love towards yourself advances your mind towards who you are in Christ.

Now, take a self-assessment to identify the depth of the love you show yourself. This is not an exercise of self-judgment. This is an exercise of edification.

Write down the answers to the following questions:

1. Are you patient with yourself?
2. Do you show kindness towards yourself when you make mistakes?
3. Do you brag about yourself or your accomplishments?
4. Do you compare your success to anyone's success while envying them?
5. Do you insist on having your way at all times?
6. Do you get angry over small issues?
7. Do you rehearse your failures and weaknesses in your mind?
8. Do you take pleasure in how God created you?
9. Are you persistent in achieving goals?
10. Do you trust yourself?

Now, take your answers from the questions and compare them to the definition of God's love found in 1 Corinthians 13:4-8 (NIV). The following illustration defines the meaning of God's love.

Compare your answers to the definition of God's love:

Patient	Kind	Always Protects	Always Trust
Always Hope	Always Persistent	Doesn't Boast (brag)	Doesn't Envy
Isn't Proud	Doesn't Dishonor Others	Not Self-Seeking	Not Easily Angered
Keeps No Record of Wrong	Doesn't Take Pleasure in Evil	Rejoices with the Truth	Love Never Fails

The love God created you in rejoices with the truth. The truth in who you were designed to be in Jesus. Remember, this is not an exercise of self-judgment. This is an exercise of edification. Receiving the truth of God's love in your heart will advance your mind towards who you are in Christ. God loves you! Jesus loves you! I love you! You love you! (smile)

Chapter 4 Summary

- Trusting God is making a commitment to allow God full access to your heart

- God looks at your heart and mind to see if you desire to do his will

- Trusting God includes edifying your mind in his knowledge

- Edification is instruction; improvement and progress of the mind, in knowledge, in morals, or in faith and holiness

- Edification includes using your conscious of being aware of who you are and where you're at in life. You awaken to your right standing with God

- Conscience is the part of your mind that knows how to put God's truth into action

- **Five ways to identify if you are committed to trusting God to edify your mind in Jesus:**

1. You allow God to instruct you on how to live your life (Psalms 32:8)

2. You receive God's word as your truth (John 17:17)

3. You allow the Holy Spirit to guide you into all truth (John 16:13)

4. You allow God's law in your mind through meditation (Joshua 1:8)

5. You put God's knowledge into action in your daily living, while discovering and experiencing the desires in your heart (James 1:22)

- Edification includes putting God's word into action with your conscience

- Jesus purged your conscience to serve God

- Conviction allow God's word to enter into your heart

- Conviction cancels self-judgment

- **Four ways to progress your mind (edify) in Christ**

  1. Keep a heart of repentance
  2. Receive power from the Holy Spirit
  3. Pray in tongues
  4. Show yourself love

A Call To Action

Love is the path to excel in every area of life. Love comes with a mindset that focuses on "being," not "doing." Love in action shows you are trusting God in every area of your life.

Self-love connects to the truth of who you were created to be. Self-love does not accept self-judgment, guilt, shame, nor low self-esteem. Instead, self-love chooses to live in the highest awareness of truth. Self-love expands through meditation. Your continued thought to love yourself elevates your mind to experience success.

Joshua 1:8 (KJV) says, "This book of the law shall not depart out of thy mouth; **but thou shalt meditate therein day and night**, that thou mayest observe to do according to all that is written therein: **for then thou shalt make thy way prosperous, and then thou shalt have good success."** Meditating on self-love is your gateway to being the best version of yourself.

Pray the following prayer:

Lord,

I am aware that loving myself is one way to trust you. I make a choice to stop self-judging myself. I release the guilt and shame that I attached to my identity. I receive your love; the love you created me to be. I ask for your strength to grow into loving myself. I thank you for the opportunity to succeed as I meditate on loving myself. I affirm that love is my path to excel in every area of my life.

In Jesus Name

Meditate

Read and meditate on 1 Corinthians 13:4-8, New International Version. I challenge you to make this your spiritual routine.

Chapter 5

Law of Human Nature

"So God created man in his own image, in the image of God created he him; male and female created he them."

Genesis 1:27 (KJV)

Human nature is the way we naturally think, feel, or act. There are many ways philosophers define human nature. The purpose of this chapter is to look at the Biblical truth regarding human nature. This chapter stands on the foundation that you were created by law in God's truth. God's word is the truth. Jesus said in John 17:17 (NIV), "Sanctify them by the truth; your word is truth."

Some laws govern how we should be citizens in the United States and other countries. God established the laws of human nature for you to be who you were created to be. You were made in God's image, which is confirmed in Genesis 1:27. Jesus is the image of God. Colossians 1:15 (NIV) says, **"The Son is the image of the invisible God, the firstborn over all creation."** This is your human nature.

Therefore, it's vital for you to know how to live by the laws of human nature to discover and live the desires in your heart. The law of gravity in simple terms is; what goes up, must come down. We make choices not to defy the law of gravity. If a ball were falling towards your head during a baseball game, you would do everything within your control to prevent the ball from falling on your head. You may get up from your seat, cover your head, or move your head around to make sure the ball doesn't fall on your head. One thing you can't do is stop the ball from falling. The ball must fall because of the law of gravity.

The Order of Human Nature

This is the same for you discovering and living the desires of your heart. You must know how the law of human nature works to experience power in God. You cannot live the desires of your heart by disregarding the law of human nature. The law of human nature is the order in which you were created, which is governed by God's truth. Your human nature includes your spirit, your soul (mind, will, and emotions) and your body. The order of your human life was designed to expand your "state of being." The first order for human beings is to live in the fullness of God's image and likeness. God designed you to thrive on living water. Living water is the life of the Lord Jesus, which is your source to live from your spirit. Yes, your spirit and soul needs God's living water for you to expand in God's image.

You are a reservoir that holds living water. You are equipped to fill the void in your heart. **A reservoir will not release water until there is a need for the water.** Living water will not flow from your heart until there is a need for it. Because you are a spiritual reservoir, you must thirst for living water to be released from your heart. Jesus said in John 7:37 (KJV), **"...If any man thirst, let him come unto me, and drink."** Thirsting for God includes having a desire to be who you were created to be in Jesus while living God's plans for your life. In John 7:38 (KJV), Jesus said, **"**He that believeth on me, as the scripture hath said, **out of his belly shall flow rivers of living water."** The Holy Spirit supplies and releases living water when you believe and thirst for Jesus. In a blog titled, "Out of Your Heart Will Flow Rivers of Living Water," John Piper shares his study on living water. His study includes the importance of living water.

Piper said, "This is the most important thing to know about yourself. You were made to live on God. You have a soul, a spirit. There is a you that is more than a body. And that you, if it does not drink from the greatness and wisdom and power and goodness and justice and holiness and love of God, will die of thirst."

Living water releases God's nature, wisdom, intellect, strength, love, etc. Therefore, you must know the "bottom line" for living water to flow from your heart. The "bottom line" is the cost. My Husband wants to know the "bottom line" before we make a purchase for the household. I will go into details about why we should make the purchase. The bottom line for living water to flow from your heart is desire. Desire is the cost you must pay. Desire is connected to your human nature. Desire is to love God with all of your heart, soul, and mind.

By the law of human nature, every person has a desire to be more. Be more than who they are. Remember what God said, "Be" fruitful, multiply, and replenish the earth." "Be" and desire are connected to your human nature.

Adam was being who he was created to be when he named the animals that God brought to him. Genesis 2:19 (KJV) says, "And out of the ground the LORD God formed every beast of the field, and every fowl of the air; and brought them unto Adam to see what he would call them: and whatsoever Adam called every living creature, that was the name thereof." This verse is an example of how human nature operates the way God intended. This verse makes it clear that God did not teach Adam what to name the animals. God did not offer an opinion on what Adam should name the animals. Instead, God brought the animals to Adam to name them. Adam was operating at the highest level of human nature. Adam's spirit, soul, and body were in oneness with God. God's divine influence on Adam's heart gave him the ability to name the animals. Adam responded to God because he had a desire to name the animals. You can operate at the highest level of your human nature when you desire to be who you were created to be in Jesus.

God designed the nature of all human beings to enjoy living by "being," not "doing." David was after God's heart. David took pleasure in God for creating him.

In Psalm 139:14 (KJV), David said, "I will praise thee; for I am fearfully and wonderfully made: marvellous are thy works; and that my soul knoweth right well." You disconnect from who you were created to be when your pleasure in "doing" exceeds your desire for "being." God desires for you to enjoy the pleasures and luxuries of life. Material possessions and life pleasures are the by-products of you "being" who you were created to be.

The same desire Adam used to name animals was the same desire that caused him to fail.

One day, a serpent got Eve's attention. This serpent used deception to communicate with Eve and deceived her to take her focus away from three essential matters. These matters were:

1. God

2. Her identity

3. God's instructions not to eat from the tree of knowledge of good and evil

All three matters are important because you need God, your identity in Christ, and God's instructions to operate at the highest level of your human nature. The serpent challenged Eve not to follow God's instructions. Eve's focus shifted towards the tree of knowledge of good and evil, which became pleasant to her eyes. Genesis 3:6 (KJV) says, "And when the woman saw that the tree was good for food, and that it was pleasant to the eyes, and a tree to be desired to make one wise, she took of the fruit thereof, and did eat, and gave also unto her husband with her; and he did eat." Eve shifted her desire from God to a tree that caused her to separate her human nature from God. Adam followed Eve with his desire and ate from the tree of knowledge of good and evil. Adam and Eve separated from the source to live in the fullness of their human nature. God gave them everything the serpent offered them.

Human Nature Separated from God

Adam and Eve's actions altered human nature. Their actions weakened and distorted human nature. Confusion and disorientation of human life continue in our time. Distort means twisted apart. Adam and Eve were twisted apart from their identity. Most importantly, they were twisted apart from God. Sorrow entered the earth and continues to have psychological effects on your mind, will, and emotions.

I usually do not discuss topics that do not progress the mind. For example, I will not write a book about depression and what it does to you. It's depressing thinking about it. Sorrow is one topic I prefer not to discuss. However, it has to be addressed to know how it blocks desires in your heart.

Sorrow seeped into your mind when something occurred that caused you pain. It will alter how you respond to people and life situations. You may have heard someone say, "I act 'this way' because 'this happened' to me." The truth is sorrow will cause you to respond to life a certain way, and you will think it's normal.

I was bullied from the time I was in first grade. I recall walking home, and a girl would intimidate me with name-calling and threats to hit me. Her actions towards me continued for several months, until one day, I had enough. I hit her as she was taunting me.

Every school year, I experienced methods of intimidations and threats from classmates. I was quiet and didn't know the students that would bully me. On the first day of school in ninth grade, I was walking into the school excited about my first day of high school. A girl who I didn't know walked up to me and said, "I'm going to kick your butt." I showed no fear of her, and she left me alone. In the tenth grade, a new student from Chicago called me derogatory names as she walked past me every day. I never introduced myself to this student and didn't have any discussion with anyone regarding her. It became very threatening when she would call my home to tell me what she was going to do to me.

I tried everything to avoid fighting this person. I was tired of fighting people for reasons that didn't matter. This is a behavior I developed to defend myself.

One day, I passed her as I was walking to class. She said to my friend, "You will need to use a towel to wipe the blood off the floor when I beat up your friend." I went to class and meditated on fighting her. I couldn't take it anymore. The bell rang, and I went after her. We fought. I sat in the Principal's office waiting for my normal consequence for fighting – a suspension.

I felt relieved. I knew she would leave me alone knowing I could beat her fighting. My Mother sat with me in the office as I waited for my suspension. The girl walked past and called me out of my name in front of my Mother. I knew then she didn't get it. My Mother looked me in the eyes and said, "You must find a better way to resolve conflict. If you don't, your suspension will turn into jail time."

A light bulb came on in my mind. I knew I wanted to go to college. Deep down, fighting was not my glory. I just used it as a tool to settle matters with people. I tell you this story because fighting was my response to the sorrow that was in my heart. I am convinced of the light skin complex in the African-American community where you experience prejudices based on your skin color from people who are African-American. The biases show in the form of competition, jealousy, envy, intimidation, gossip, etc. I experienced conflict for invalid reasons. The sorrow of being bullied came with the pain of rejection, oppression, and anger. I accepted this as being standard in my life.

Here is the truth about sorrow; it will cause you to think it is normal. I stopped fighting. I reacted a different way to intimidation, wrongdoing, and insults against me. This different way was not the right way. I would attempt to avoid confrontation when I would experience any form of injustice. My reaction to injustice would turn into aggression when my back was against the wall. I would respond to people with anger. I would give people a "piece of my mind." I built walls around me where I could not get out nor let people in. My reaction to life was; I would not let anyone hurt me. This was my mantra. I kept this attitude in college, in my career and relationships, while having a relationship with God.

Sorrow is a silent epidemic that has affected cultures, families, races, and genders. African-Americans deal with sorrow that comes from slavery, segregation, hate crimes, racism, etc. Anger is an issue of pain, not a matter of weakness or incompetence. It's an issue of not being acknowledged for identity, strengths, talents, influence, values, courage, motherhood, fatherhood, etc. As an African-American woman in school, college, and my career, I wasn't allowed to "Be" who I was created to be.

Instead, I heard, *you are not good enough* in many forms of communication. I remember being totally ignored my first time attending a predominantly white school in the sixth grade. All of my teachers were Caucasian at this school. I had six teachers. Not one teacher engaged me in the classroom for my first week. I didn't return to school for a week because I was dealing with the culture shock of not being accepted. I felt like I didn't have the competence to learn the teachers' style of teaching. This is a school district where African-American students were threatened with racial hate by Caucasian students in the late '80s and early '90s. The school administration showed no concern until I was in the tenth grade.

In college, I was told by my guidance counselor my junior year that I was not competent to graduate. I knew then she didn't look at my academic record because I received mostly As, while majoring in Social Work. It was the most prejudice statement I heard. I graduated from college because I had the desire to obtain a degree.

In my career, I came to work joyful and ready to start my day. A supervisor came to me and asked me to work on a case for an absent co-worker. I calmly told him I would look at the case once I get settled. I was waiting for my computer to boot as I was talking to him. He aggressively grabbed my chair while I was sitting in it and said, "You will do it now." His response to me was very aggressive. It was disturbing to experience how the department covered his behavior. I wasn't the only employee he was aggressive towards. The best solution my department suggested in handling this matter was for me to transfer. He apologized for his actions towards me six years later.

The point I'm making is there are battles you experienced most of your life to just "Be." The battles are ways sorrow attach to your mind, will, and emotions. I mentioned sorrow earlier in this book, but I wanted to show how sorrow connects to your human nature. You will spend most of your life dancing with sorrow, thinking you are not good enough. Therefore, it's nothing wrong with you. God provides living water for you to move past anything that opposes the truth of who you were created to be. I made the decision to release the tools I used to defend myself. God didn't create you to defend yourself with anger, competition, intimidation, deceit, emotional eating, bitterness, manipulation, controlling others, aggression, passiveness, etc. God created you to be your defender. Psalm 62:1-2 (KJV) says, "Truly my soul waiteth upon God: from him cometh my salvation.[2] He only is my rock and my salvation; he is my defence; I shall not be greatly moved."

God restored dominion to you when he made you a new creation. He gave you dominion over sorrow. Sorrow is a sign that you need God. Pause for a moment and take in the truth that it is illegal for you to carry sorrow, issues, and your responses to what caused you to act the way you do. Why? Jesus paid the price for you **NOT** to live according to what happened to you. You may have been adopted, abused, molested, forsaken by your Mother or Father, misunderstood, bullied, rejected, discriminated against, etc. This is not part of your human nature. Your identity stands alone. Your identity is God's image. This means your image is separate from your race, family, culture, society, people's expectations of you, etc. Jesus didn't open his mouth while he paid the price for you to have your identity reconciled to God. Adam's sin separated you from God; Jesus sacrificed his life and returned you to God. 2 Corinthians 5:19 (NIV) says, "that God was reconciling the world to himself in

Christ, not counting people's sins against them. And he has committed to us the message of reconciliation." This book is my message to encourage you to reconcile your human nature to God. When you accepted Jesus as your Savior and Lord, sorrow no longer had the rights to be in your heart.

New Creation

You are a new creation in Christ. This is a law of human nature for every believer of Jesus Christ. Do you believe it? You must believe it to experience your newness in Christ. Your spirit is new, but your soul is restored through Christ. Psalm 23:3 (KJV) says, "He restoreth my soul: he leadeth me in the paths of righteousness for his name's sake." The restoration of your soul is engaging your human nature in God's truth. This starts with living from the foundation of who you are. The foundation of your human nature is your spirit. You live from your spiritual nature, which is your identity in Christ. Your natural mind doesn't know your identity in Christ nor God's plans for your life. Only the spirit of God can reveal this to you.

This is where people get confused about knowing their purpose. "What is my purpose?" is the million-dollar question many people cannot answer. 1 Corinthians 2:9

(NIV) says, **"However, as it is written: "What no eye has seen, what no ear has heard, and what no human mind has conceived" the things God has prepared for those who love him."** What God has for you is connected to your spirit. This is why people may get a career, get married, go shopping, travel, join social organizations and continue to feel a void in their hearts.

I studied the behavior of athletes for two years. My natural mind believed that my purpose was to serve professional athletes. My natural mind was wrong. There is a pattern of seeing talented players with amazing skills and abilities. Their intelligence is at the highest level when it comes to sports, but they have challenges engaging people with character and values. This doesn't make them incompetent to reach their potential. It merely means they are incomplete. What makes athletes incomplete?

They are engaging in life based on their talent. Athletes' physical strengths are applauded before they develop in character, logical thinking, managing emotions, etc. Their physical nature looks sharp, but you cannot see the deficiency they experience with their self-image. This is the same for you. You can't live on your talent alone. You must know your spiritual foundation to get the big picture of who you are. Your image, talent, and influence are included in your spiritual foundation. Your spiritual foundation is released through your soul.

Here is the big picture of who you were created to be:

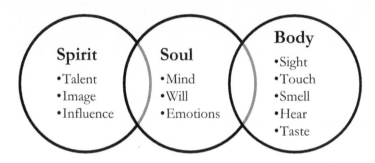

This your truth being purpose-driven. It's your foundation to live in the fullness of God's image and plans for your life. This is your ground to produce desires from your heart.

I mentioned before that Jesus chose and appointed you to produce fruit. Fruit are the results of how you live your life daily. I mentioned how I thought life was a buffet of options when it came to fulfilling goals. I knew that God would be there for me to support my decisions. I foolishly thought that God was my "get out of jail" God. So, I would hastily make decisions, act, then pray nothing goes wrong. This is illegal for human nature. My choices were not connected to what God chose and appointed me to do. Jesus chose and appointed you to produce fruit from your foundation.

God did not appoint me to work my entire life in my career. I kept working and praying for promotions. An opportunity came that appeared to be a breakthrough to expand my talent and skill set. Things were going well. I was assigned to work with the central administration team. Also, I was assigned to a project with the State administration. I connected to my hidden potential and was thriving.

One day, I received notice unexpectedly that I was assigned back to my previous position. Immediately, my confidence went from 10 to 0. Depression flooded my soul like a Tsunami. I was wondering where God was in this. I believe God is a God of progress, not regress. God removed me from this assignment because it wasn't connected to what Jesus chose me to do.

Here is the truth, I was not connected to my foundation that includes my image, talent, and influence. The season of my career was over, but I couldn't make the connection because I had a distorted connection with my job.

Your spirit is a new creation, but your soul is dealing with the psychology of life. You have to live from your spirit to live in the newness of who you are in Christ. Your mind, will, and emotions cannot process the "new you" because it is separate from your spirit. So, when God is connecting to your desire, it's static interference. It's like listening to a radio station with static. You can't hear the music clearly — the reason there is static because your intellectual faculties are separate from God's intellect. You can't live from your spiritual foundation when you are twisted apart from your human nature. Your spirit, soul, body are not in harmony. You correct this by connecting your intellectual faculties with God's truth. He created you in truth because all his works are done in truth. Psalms 33:4 (KJV) says, "For the word of the LORD is right; and all his works are done in truth." God's word is your truth to using your intellectual faculties. This is part of trusting God.

You have six intellectual faculties that are connected to your understanding of learning, making decisions, and taking action. Proverbs 3:5 (KJV) says, **"Trust in the LORD with all thine heart; and lean not unto thine own understanding."** Your six intellectual faculties are for you to produce your fruit in God's truth. The six intellectual faculties are imagination, intuition, memory, perception, reasoning, and will. Adam used all six of his, the way God intended them to be used before he ate of the tree of knowledge of good and evil. Now, let's look at all six intellectual faculties according to God's word.

1. Imagination

Imagination is the part of your intellect that conceives and form images or ideas in your mind. The 1828 Webster dictionary defines it as the first purpose of your mind. Adam was able to name the animals God brought to him with his imagination. God gave Adam the idea to name the animals. Psalm 33:11 (KJV) says, **"The counsel of the LORD standeth for ever, the thoughts of his heart to all generations."** Adam was connected with God when he received the imagination from God to name the animals. God is the source of your imagination.

Your imagination is used for but not limited to the following:

- To have an image of who you are in Christ
- To use your talent
- To use your influence
- To know the details of God's plans for your life
- To keep good and pure thoughts

God repented and was grieved that He made humans when he saw people use their imagination for evil. Genesis 6:5-6 (KJV) says, "And God saw that the wickedness of man was great in the earth, and that every imagination of the thoughts of his heart was only evil continually. 6 And it repented the LORD that he had made man on the earth, and it grieved him at his heart." This is deep. Meditating on that alone is sobering. The use of imagination was far from God after the fall of mankind.

This is why it is important to be attentive when God gives you an idea. This is God's way of partnering with you to advance your mind, potential, talent, influence, etc., also being a solution for people who need your service.

2. Intuition

Joshua Parker started making maple syrup at eleven years old. He decided he wanted to make maple syrup after a field trip-learning about maple syrup. He started making small batches and opened a maple business at fifteen years old. This started with his intuition to make maple syrup. Joshua Parker said, "We believe in pushing the boundaries to find the ultimate good, the ultimate great, that brings us to who we were all created to be. We believe that there's inherent goodness in pushing yourself further than you thought imaginable, and then looking back on what you accomplished with courage, proudness, and humility."

Intuition is your intellectual faculty to have direct knowledge without evidence. Adam used his intuition on naming the animals. Educational institutions were not available to give Adam insight about naming animals. This is the same when it comes to parenting. A Mother and Father have an intuition on raising their children. Their intuition kicks in the moment they become parents.

Job 38:36 (NLT) says, **"Who gives intuition to the heart and instinct to the mind?"** God gave you an intuition to fulfill his plans for your life. Your intuition is connected to your talent. I recall sitting in sessions of the mentoring group I coordinated, noticing how my intuition was connected to the knowledge of human behavior and potential. The understanding of how our potential expands in a personal growth environment.

My intuition allowed me to create content without specialized training to present to a skill trade school. This was before I was certified to be a Trainer, Speaker, and Coach. Exodus 35:35 (NLT) says, "The LORD has given them special skills as engravers, designers, embroiderers in blue, purple, and scarlet thread on fine linen cloth, and weavers. They excel as craftsmen and as designers." God gives you special skills through intuition. What are the unique skills that you use through your intuition?

3. Memory

You prepared for the test you have taken by memorizing the information. You pass the test, but you don't remember what was on the test. Your memory didn't keep the information on the test. Memory is a function in your mind that keep a record of past events or an idea. Your memory is key to you living in the truth of who you were created to be in Jesus. Do you keep in your memory the truth of who you are?

Sorrow causes you to go down memory lane to reflect on past events. Isaiah 43:18 (KJV) says, **"Remember ye not the former things, neither consider the things of old."** Once you keep your memory on past events, you regress in living. This causes you to attach your self-judgment, negative emotions, failures, weakness, or bad habits to your identity. You forget who you are in Christ when you keep memories of the past. God holds the truth of who He created you to be in His memory. You are complete in Christ. Colossians 2:9-10 (KJV) says, "For in him dwelleth all the fulness of the Godhead bodily. [10] And ye are complete in him, which is the head of all principality and power:" There is nothing defective about you.

Meditating on God's word will keep your memory in God's truth. Therefore, it's essential to allow God's word to invade your mind daily. 1 Corinthians 15:2 (KJV) says, "By which also ye are saved, if ye keep in memory what I preached unto you, unless ye have believed in vain." Keeping God's word in your memory includes putting God's knowledge into action. Your memory allows God's truth to govern your life in "real time," minute by minute.

4. Perception

Perception is how you view yourself and your life. This includes how you see God, people, circumstances, etc. You cannot move forward in your life without the accurate perception of who you are in Christ. Your perception matters.

Jesus asked his disciples, "Whom do men say that I am?" The disciples gave different answers. Some said Jesus was John the Baptist, Elijah, or Jeremiah. Peter gave Jesus the correct answer. Matthew 16:16 (KJV) says, "And Simon

Peter answered and said, Thou art the Christ, the Son of the living God." Peter's answer was based on his perception. Who was the source of Peter's perception? God. Matthew 16:17 (NIV) says, "Jesus replied, "Blessed are you, Simon son of Jonah, for this was not revealed to you by flesh and blood, but by my Father in heaven."

God is your source for your perception when it comes to being who you were created to be. People cannot reveal to you what Jesus chose and appointed you to do. Your five senses of touch, sight, sound, smell, or taste cannot help you identify God's plans for your life. This is all based on living from your spirit. Colossians 1:9-10 (KJV) says, "For this cause we also, since the day we heard it, do not cease to pray for you, and to desire that ye might be filled with the knowledge of his will in all wisdom and spiritual understanding;[10] That ye might walk worthy of the Lord unto all pleasing, being fruitful in every good work, and increasing in the knowledge of God;" Using your perception requires having wisdom and spiritual understanding in the knowledge of God.

5. Reason

God instructed me to partner with a church to coordinate a mentoring group at a public high school. My reason for organizing the mentoring group was based on my faith in God. My supervisor was not in agreement with my idea. Her reasoning was based on the societal norm of separation of church and state.

Reasoning is your thinking headquarters. It is a faculty of your mind that draws conclusions about God, yourself, people, circumstances, truth, facts, good, evil, etc. You have a reason for doing everything you do. Your reasoning could be based on how you were raised, societal norms, laws, people opinion, circumstances, etc. Your reason is connected to what you think. Therefore, there is a reason to how you live your life daily. There is no gray area in what you are thinking.

Think of a time when you asked a person, "why did you do that." Their response was, "I don't know." They gave you their honest response, but the truth is there is a reason for their action. They were not aware of how a certain way they think is connected to their actions. Their thinking is limited in a certain area of their life. I call it "controlled thinking." Controlled thinking is thinking based on facts, people, customs, traditions, limitations, etc. This type of thinking doesn't accept who you were created to be. Controlled thinking comes with labels, oppression, negativity, toxic relationship or fears which disconnect you from the desires of your heart. This is important to know because the desires of your heart are connected to "independent thinking."

Independent thinking is thinking free of logic and limitations. This type of thinking is based on faith in God and His word. God wants you to reason with him. God said in Isaiah 1:18 (KJV), "**Come now, and let us reason together, saith the LORD:** though your sins be as scarlet, they shall be as white as snow; though they be red like crimson, they shall be as wool." Your reasoning must include faith in your thinking that is free of logic and limitations.

6. Will

For many years, I would make a choice, but there were no actions connected to it. I lacked the will to act on the choices I made in the past. The will is an intellectual faculty to take action. Your will starts with a choice. The choice is incomplete without using your will to take action.

You are familiar with the saying, "actions speak louder than words." Your will are actions that speak louder than what you say.

Therefore, your will requires an expression of what you perceive, imagine, reason, or memorize driven by your intuition. Jesus said he choose and appointed you. Jesus wants to know if you are **ALL IN** with your six intellectual faculties. Your will identifies if you are all in. Jesus paid the price for your sorrow with his will. Jesus said in Luke 22:42 (KJV), "Saying, Father, if thou be willing, remove this cup from me: nevertheless not my will, but thine, be done." Jesus aligned his will with God's will for his life.

Your will signifies that you are owning your truth. You must do the following to live in the truth of your human nature:

1. Own Your Truth

What is your truth? What do you live by every day? How do you experience freedom "to be"? Jesus paid the price for your freedom. Galatians 5:1 (NIV) says, "It is for freedom that Christ has set us free. Stand firm, then, and do not let yourselves be burdened again by a yoke of slavery." Your freedom is connected to you owning your truth. How do you own your truth? Owning your truth start with putting into practice Jesus' teaching. Jesus said in John 8:31-32 (KJV), "If ye continue in my word, then are ye my disciples indeed; And ye shall know the truth, and the truth shall make you free."

Ownership comes with accountability. A person that owns a home takes pride in what they own. They willfully take on the responsibility to have dominion over their house. You lease yourself out to everything that is against who you were created to be when you don't own your truth. In other words, you give up your legal right to have dominion over who you were designed to be in Christ. Owning your truth is closing the door to a life that produces unsatisfying results.

Haggai 1:6 (KJV) says, "You have planted much, but harvested little. You eat, but never have enough. You drink, but never have your fill. You put on clothes, but are not warm. You earn wages, only to put them in a purse with holes in it." Leasing your truth yields little to no results. You must examine areas of your life where you are not owning your truth. Haggai 1:7 (KJV) says, **"Thus saith the LORD of hosts; Consider your ways."** Examining your human nature starts with the foundation of who you are. You examine your foundation with your spiritual mind.

Here are examples of owning your truth vs. leasing your truth:

Owning Your Truth

- Receive God's Instructions
- Single Mind
- Focused
- Embrace Change
- Teachable
- Open Mind = Knowledge
- Creative = Work Smarter with Results
- Intentional About Living
- Grateful
- Satisfied
- Persistent
- Authentic Image = Value Self

Leasing Your Truth

- Reject God's Instructions
- Double Mind
- Distracted
- Reject Change
- Not Teachable
- Close Mind = Reject Knowledge
- Compete = Work Hard with Few Results
- Accept Life As-Is
- Complain
- Not Satisfied
- Procrastinate
- Distored Image = Compare Self to Others

2. Become Spiritually Minded

Being spiritually minded helps you discover your desires. A person with a spiritual mindset builds their life on the revelation of God's word. I read horoscopes in the newspaper when I was a teenager. I would read it to see what it would say about my future. Only the Holy Spirit is to lead you into all truth. Anything else that invade, your mind, will, and emotions are illegal. Deuteronomy 18:9-13 (NIV) says, "When you enter the land the LORD your God is giving you, do not learn to imitate the detestable ways of the nations there. [10] Let no one be found among you who sacrifices their son or daughter in the fire, who practices divination or sorcery, interprets omens, engages in witchcraft,[11] or casts spells, or who is a medium or spiritist or who consults the dead. [12] Anyone who does these things is detestable to the LORD; because of these same detestable practices, the LORD your God will drive out those nations before you. [13] You must be blameless before the LORD your God." The revelation of God's word reveals the truth about your desires and future.

You become spiritually minded when you see yourself in God's word. Therefore, you must find yourself in God's word by faith. Jesus went to the synagogue in

Nazareth. He read Isaiah 61:1, which is a prophecy of him being in the earth. Jesus found himself in the scripture. Luke 4:21 (KJV) says, "And he began to say unto them, 'This day is this scripture fulfilled in your ears." The people in the synagogue did not recognize Jesus with their natural mind. Jesus had a spiritual mindset to see who he was in the scriptures.

You experience regeneration when you become spiritually minded. Titus 3:5 (KJV) says, "Not by works of righteousness which we have done, but according to his mercy he saved us, by the washing of regeneration, and renewing of the Holy Ghost;"

Reproduction is one word that defines regeneration. You become reproduced in who you were created to be when you have a spiritual mindset. You experience the "true" nature of who you are. Here is the secret to building your spiritual mind. Be "all in" with your mind. How often do you read your Bible? I intend not to be offensive in any way. This is a spiritual lifestyle. What you do daily determines how effective you will be to live the desires from your heart.

The Book of Acts provides truth to Holy Spirit empowering people who were motivated to fulfill God's purpose. The disciples were thrust into being leaders. There were two groups of Jews who heard the message on Jesus Christ. The first group were jealous and did not believe Paul. The second group believed Paul and received God's word with readiness of mind. They read the scriptures daily. Acts 17:11 (KJV) says, "These were more noble than those in Thessalonica, in that they received the word with all readiness of mind, and searched the scriptures daily, whether those things were so." This is the same for you. A readiness in your mind to search the scriptures daily is required to live at the highest level of your human nature.

Chapter 5 Summary

- You must know how the law of human nature works to experience desires in your heart
- The law of human nature is the order in which you were created, which is governed by God's truth
- Living water is the life of the Lord Jesus, which is your source to live from your spirit
- Living water releases God's nature, wisdom, intellect, strength, love, etc.
- You were created by law in God's truth
- Human nature is the way you naturally think, feel, or act
- Your spirit, soul (mind, will, emotions), and body is the structure of your human nature
- Your spirit is the foundation of your "state of being"
- Your human nature has a desire to be more by law
- The desire for the tree of knowledge of good and evil separated mankind from God and the truth of their human nature
- You are a new creation when you accept Jesus as your Lord and Savior
- **Your soul must be restored by God's word, including your six intellectual faculties:**
    1. Imagination
    2. Intuition

3. Memory
4. Perception
5. Reasoning
6. Will

- Owning your truth is living by the truth of God's word
- Become spiritually minded to see yourself in God's word

A Call To Action

Your human nature works in God's truth. You were made by a God of perfection. Everything about who he created you to be is perfected in Jesus Christ.

God knew you wouldn't understand how to live the way you were created. This is why he sent Jesus into the earth to sacrifice his life, so that you may live your life in freedom. This is not automatic. This happens when you seek God's will for your life in all wisdom and spiritual understanding. God wants you to live with the lights on at all time. Ephesians 1:18 (KJV) says, "**The eyes of your understanding being enlightened**; that ye may know what is the hope of his calling, and what the riches of the glory of his inheritance in the saints," This means he wants you to see more clearly knowledge and understanding regarding his truth about you.

Pray the following prayer:

Lord,

I ask that you give me spiritual understanding and wisdom to know your will for my life. Help me to see clearly every detail about my human nature connected to my freedom in Jesus Christ. I don't take for granted all that you created me to be. I show my appreciation, seeking and living your will for my life. Thank you for creating me in your truth.

In Jesus Name.

Meditate
Read and meditate on Ephesians 1:17-19. These scriptures are a prayer for getting clarity, wisdom, and understanding into knowledge about God and his power in you.

Chapter 6

The Mind of Christ

"For who hath known the mind of the Lord, that he may instruct him? but we have the mind of Christ."

1 Corinthians 2:16 (KJV)

"You are what you think." This is not a cliché. This is the truth. What do you think of yourself? Proverbs 23:7 (KJV) says, **"For as he thinketh in his heart, so is he:"** Do you think of your failures, weakness, or qualifications? I was withdrawn during my first years of elementary school. My teachers became concerned and began testing me for special education. I wasn't placed in special education, but barely passed math and science. I thrived in music and sports.

I continued to struggle in academics when I attended a predominately Caucasian middle school. I stopped playing the flute because I didn't fit in. I was intimidated by the culture. I wouldn't attempt to engage my classes when they were challenging.

My sister graduated from high school and went to college. I became determined to do my best because I wanted to go to college too, so I engaged my academics.

At the start of my senior year, I only applied to one college. I didn't think I would be accepted at other colleges, and I wanted to stay close to home. I was accepted at Eastern Michigan University under one condition that I complete the Summer Incentive Program. I completed the program, but I continued to be affected by how I viewed my weaknesses.

The pattern of being intimidated by predominately Caucasian schools worsened even more. I wouldn't engage classes that challenged my thinking. I avoided taking classes that I thought were "hard." I remember taking Psychology 101. This class was challenging, yet it was intriguing. I enjoyed my study time even though the concepts were "foreign" to me. I got an A in that class.

I majored in social work because of my thinking. I thought I would succeed in the courses related to social work, and I successfully received my degree.

James Allen says, "A man is literally what he thinks, his character being the complete sum of his thoughts." Here is the lead-in. I chose a career based on what I thought.

I had faith for a career that I knew I could do well in. I never asked God what his plans were. I chose what my mind conceived at the time. Your desires are not connected to what your mind can conceive. Your spiritual mind only knows the desires in your heart. Your mind is closed to any desire you think are beyond your capabilities. This will cause you to attach your vision to what you think you qualify for. You will keep looking for jobs that match your past. The fact is your past is attached to your educational experiences, failures, weakness, qualifications, past success, or job title. This is why it is challenging for a person to discover their purpose.

The truth is the work Jesus appointed you to do has nothing to do with your educational experiences, failures, weakness, qualifications, past success, or job titles. How do you change your thinking to do the work you were chosen for? You receive the mind of Christ.

God created you to live from your spirit, which is the foundation of who you are. This means God has given you everything you need to live from your spirit. God gifted you with a mind to fulfill your mission in life. You were gifted you with the mind of Christ.

There are three areas that are connected to your spirit. They are your image, talent, and influence. You

CANNOT discover your desires nor live them without these authentic areas. You are out of rhythm with God giving you the desires of your heart when they are not in use. They are all connected to your potential. This is why 70% of Americans are not engaging but dreading their careers. They are not in harmony being who God created them to be. This is a human epidemic — definitely, a Christian epidemic.

We were trained to "get a job" vs. doing what we are called to do. Yes, we should get a job, but employment is sought based on salary, social trends, or what a person thinks they can do.

I grew up in and near Flint, Michigan from the late '70s thru the mid '90s. The trend was to work at General Motors. A family member, friend of the family, classmate's parent, church members, community organizer, etc. worked at General Motors. Majority of GM workers disregarded their talent to support their family. There were GM workers who just used their talent as a side job but kept GM as their main source of income. This is an example of how people discard their talent and God's plans for their lives. The truth remains that your first priority must be to God. Did you make God the first priority to using your talent and influence?

I sought God, regarding his plans for my life. He instructed me to quit my job. As I drove to work, I kept hearing his inner voice to quit my job. I continued to ignore it.

One day, this decision fell on me like a ton of bricks. I had the desire to quit. The Mind of Christ was operating in my life.

The disciples made a connection with "truth," which was God seeking expression through them. The truth hidden in your heart is a force. It's God seeking a greater expression of who you are in him. God is looking to see if you will make him a priority. Jesus chose and appointed them to be disciples. What did Jesus appoint you to do? Have you responded with your heart? Now, I'm **NOT TELLING YOU TO QUIT YOUR JOB. I DON'T RECOMMEND QUITTING YOUR JOB. I'M ENCOURAGING YOU TO DO WHAT GOD HAS CHOSEN YOU TO DO.** God instructed me to quit my job to receive his instructions about my calling. I was thinking through the mind of Christ. God's truth overrides logic. The mind of Christ comes with God's instructions.

I Corinthians 2:16 (KJV) says, "For who has known the mind of the LORD that he may instruct Him? But we have the mind of Christ."

What is the Mind of Christ?

The mind of Christ is a mindset to release God's power through your mind. God's power works in the conscience part of the mind. Jesus used His mind to release God's spirit to remove burdens and destroy yokes (bondage). Isaiah 10:27 (KJV) says, "And it shall come to pass in that day, that his burden shall be taken away from off thy shoulder, and his yoke from off thy neck, and **the yoke shall be destroyed because of the anointing."**

A burden is anything that weighs you down. A yoke is anything that has you in bondage from being who you were created to "be" while living God's plans for your life. Christ means the anointed; Jesus is the Anointed One. The spirit of the Lord anointed Jesus to fulfill His ministry on the earth. Acts 10:38 (KJV) says, "How **God anointed Jesus of Nazareth** with the Holy Ghost and with power: who went about doing good, and healing all that were oppressed of the devil; for God was with him." Jesus' mind was anointed by God to demonstrate God's power over the law of human nature. This is the mind of Christ.

The mind is not the brain. The brain is the organ. The mind is the pure intention of a person. The mind is where your intention, will and desire are enforced. For example, a police officer job is to enforce the law. A police officer is enforcing the law when they issue a ticket to a person driving over the speed limit. Your mind enforces your motive through your intentions.

God intended for you to use your mind to enforce his truth in your life. This includes being who you were created to be while executing his plans. The mind of Christ was a mindset Jesus had to be the Son of God in the earth. Jesus used his mind a certain way to carry out God's plans. Jesus intention, will, and desire was to correct Adam's costly mistake. Jesus' mind displayed his intentions for being the gift to the world. His intention of being Savior and Lord to all people. To give everyone the opportunity to receive eternal life.

Jesus' mind was connected to "being" the Son of God and God's plan for His life on earth. John 3:16 (KJV), "**For God so loved the world, that he gave his only begotten Son, that whosoever believeth in him should not perish, but have everlasting life.**"

Jesus' intention, will, and desire was in "being" the following:

- The Word (John 1:1)
- All things being made by him (John 1:3)

- He is the life source that is the light of all humans (John 1:4)
- His light shined in darkness: (John 1:5)
- He gives power for us to become the children of God (John 1:12)
- He is the Word made into flesh (John 1:14)
- He came with grace and truth (John 1:17)

Jesus' mind was driven by one mission; to please the Father. He made sure his mind was aligned with God's intention, will, and desire for "being" the Son of God. Jesus had to follow the laws of human nature to fulfill this mission. He came as man in the fullness of God's image. Jesus is the only person that walked the earth in the fullness of God. This is called the deity. The deity is the Godhead. Colossians 2:9 (KJV) says, "For in him dwelleth all the fulness of the Godhead bodily." Jesus made the sacrifice by giving up his divine nature for human nature. A mindset comes with sacrifice.

The Mind of Christ Method

What is your method of operation? The response to this question should include the way you live your life. Jesus had a method for living on the earth. Knowledge was Jesus' method to use His mind with the full intention to give life.

Isaiah 53:11 (KJV) says, "He shall see of the travail of his soul, and shall be satisfied: **by his knowledge shall my righteous servant justify many;** for he shall bear their iniquities." Jesus' human nature needed knowledge for his mind. Therefore, Jesus was intentional to get knowledge. The mind expands with knowledge. The mind operates either out of knowledge or ignorance. What would life be like if Jesus failed in his mission? What if Jesus' response for failing was "I didn't know?" He left no room for failure. Jesus knew his first order was to get knowledge. There is no grey area with the use of the mind. Jesus' mind needed knowledge to put into action God's plans. This is the reason he was found learning in the temple at the age of 12.

What type of knowledge did Jesus get? He received God's knowledge to live life. The knowledge to live in the fullness of God on the earth. Isaiah 11:2 (KJV) says, "And the spirit of the LORD shall rest upon him, the spirit of wisdom and understanding, the spirit of counsel and might, the spirit of knowledge and of the fear of the LORD;" God's wisdom, understanding, counsel, power, and honor rested on Jesus. God's intellect expanded in Jesus' mind when Jesus submitted to get knowledge. God's spirit rested on Jesus while he received God's teachings. This caused Jesus to increase in wisdom. Luke 2:52 (KJV), "**And Jesus increased in wisdom and stature, and in favor with God and man.**" Jesus' intention to get knowledge equipped his mind for his intention, will, and desire to "be" the Son of God and live God's plans for his life.

God is the source to "being" who you were created to be. God and Jesus connected mentally. The mind of God gave the mind of Christ instructions to fulfill his mission on earth came.

Remember 1 Corinthians 2:16 (KJV):
"For who hath known the mind of the Lord, that he may instruct him? but we have the mind of Christ."

Jesus made sure his mind was not tainted with outside influences. This is the reason I pray over myself and family that no ungodly influences penetrate our minds. One definition of 'penetrate' is to affect the mind. Jesus allowed God to affect his mind. He boldly proclaimed that his teachings came from God. John 7:16 (NIV) says, **"Jesus answered, 'My teaching is not my own. It comes from the one who sent me.'"**

Every action Jesus took was based on God's teachings. The mind of Christ is a mindset that lives by God's teachings. Jesus' mindset included knowledge on how to put God's truth into action. This is a method that Jesus made available to you when you received him as your Lord and Savior. Jesus was strategic in having a mindset to receive God's teachings. Jesus did not use his divine nature to his advantage. Jesus strategically put into action the following:

- Jesus gave up his divine nature (Philippians 2:6)
- Jesus became a man by nature (Philippians 2:7)
- Jesus gave up his rights as the Son of God (Philippians 2:7)
- Jesus made himself a person with no reputation (Philippians 2:7)
- Jesus acknowledged that he was a servant in human nature (Philippians 2:7)
- Jesus humbled himself (Philippians 2:8)
- Jesus became obedient to death, including death on the cross (Philippians 2:8)

This is the reason you have the ability to be like Jesus.

This strategy is a blueprint for you to put into action what Jesus chose and appointed you to do. You are to do it through the mind of Christ. Philippians 2:5 (KJV) says, **"Let this mind be in you, which was also in Christ Jesus:"** Let the mind of Christ penetrate your mind. You were given a mind to produce what Jesus chose and appointed you to do. Consider the following when discovering what Jesus chose and appointed you to do:

1. Who you are in Christ
2. Your talents
3. Your influence
4. The problems you are called to solve

I studied athletes' behavior for two years. There was a study completed by the National Longitudinal Study of Adolescent Health, on more than 6,000 male students from 120 schools.

One of the conclusions from this study revealed Forty Percent of football players were more likely to be in a confrontation than non-athletes. I wanted to know why their negative behavior exceeds their talent. All talent is a gift from God. Every person was born with one or more talents.

How we use or don't use our talent is not a defect by God. I wanted to know from God's word the solution to having success with athletes' talent.

Talent comes from your spirit. Your spiritual foundation includes your image, talent, and influence. You need them to succeed. Your image is a representation of your mind. This includes what you think, perceive, memorize, reason, will, believe, etc. Leadership is influence. You were born a leader.

When an athlete is born, their talent is displayed more than their image and influence. The reason being their talent is displayed with their body. We see with our eyes their strengths, not their weakness. We don't see the low self-esteem or inability to connect with people. The truth remains that athletes were made in God's image with talent and influence. You were born a leader in God's image and likeness. You were given a talent to provide a solution to the world.

The solution to the athletes' behavior is to nurture their image and influence with their talent. The solution for you to put into action what you were chosen to do is to nurture your image, talent, and influence. You may have the strength to connect with people. My influence needed nurturing. I didn't know how to connect with people who were different from me. I think "black and white" according to God's truth. This is one of my talents to discern God's truth, but I needed to nurture my influence in God's love. Therefore, you must let the mind of Christ expand in your mind to nurture your image, talent, and influence. You cannot do it this with your natural mind.

"Look the part" is what I heard throughout my life. I "looked the part" most of my life with low self-esteem. God challenged me to live what I learned after I prayed for credibility. God put me in the mirror, which is the word of God to examine myself.

1 Corinthians 11:28 (KJV) says, **"But let a man examine himself, and so let him eat of that bread, and drink of that cup."** One duty of a follower of Jesus is to partake of the Lord's supper. This is an act of faith to keep in remembrance Jesus dying for you. The purpose of this is to examine yourself. You examine your lifestyle as a Christian. This includes examining your image, talent, and influence. Here is what God examines in your heart:

1. What Is On Your Mind?

Your **image** represents what you think. God wants to know if you have a mindset to act like him. This mindset is covered in humility. Humility is having a mindset without pride or arrogance. A mindset covered in humility submits to the divine will of God. Jesus' strategy to keep a mindset of humility was to be a person of no reputation. Jesus didn't consider his reputation while being intentional to please God.

Things were going well when I started with the John Maxwell Team. The second year took a turn. Potential contracts failed, and I was not getting clients. I heard a lot of no, no, no, no, no, no, no, and, no. This means our finances were in the red. I debated attending a John Maxwell Team local meeting. I was ashamed of my financial situation. I knew I would hear success stories and I didn't have a story to share. I didn't have five dollars to pay for lunch.

I woke up that morning and made the decision to go in my truth. The truth is my image is not to "look the part." My image is being who I was created to be. I went in with no reputation. I showed up in humility. I paid for my lunch with mostly coins. I sat knowing me "being" was pleasing God while being in his divine will. Your image is about you "being" in good times and bad times while being intentional in submitting to God's divine will. The desires in your heart are connected to you being a person of no reputation.

2. Where is Your Talent?

God examines your heart to see if you are using your **talent**. Your talent is produced from your heart. It is connected to desires in the heart. God looked at David's heart before David was anointed as king. One of the reasons David was chosen is because he produced his talents from his heart. David had the talent to take care of sheep and play the harp. His talent was connected to him being King. Matthew 25:14-29 provides the truth on using what you have. The story provides an example with the use of money. It shares a revelation about talent and capitalism. All the people were given talents according to their ability. The person that was given one talent hid it because he was afraid. The person with the one talent excuse caused him to lose his talent. This sounds cruel, but this is a life principle about putting to use what God has given you. What you don't use, you lose. Jesus' strategy for using talent was obedience. Philippians 2:8 (KJV) says, **"And being found in fashion as a man, he humbled himself, and became obedient unto death, even the death of the cross."**

Jesus' talent was using knowledge to sacrifice his life. He became obedient to give his life unto death. **The key to using your talent is obedience**. Benjamin Banneker was a man that put his talent to use. He was an author, scientist, mathematician, farmer, astronomer, publisher, and urban planner. He invented a wooden clock that was accurate in providing time. Banneker published six almanacs in twenty-eight editions. He played a major role as a surveyor for Washington D.C. This is astounding because he was self-taught. Banneker taught himself astronomy and advanced math. Your talent flourishes with the desires of your heart. This comes with you being obedient with your talent.

3. How Are You Connecting with People?

Nothing can be accomplished without **influence**. My mentor, John C. Maxwell, provided the best definition for leadership. He says, "Leadership is influence, nothing more, nothing less."

God examines how you connect with people with your influence. You have influence with people you are connected to. Leadership is not a title; leadership is connecting with people. Influence is not neutral. The greatest demonstration of connecting with people was when Jesus washed the disciples' feet in John 13. Jesus is the word in flesh. Jesus used his influence by washing feet. Feet represent daily living. Jesus was intentional to wash their feet to show how his influence affects their daily living. Your influence is either positive or negative. God looks at your heart to see if you are connecting with people with love. Jesus' strategy for using influence was being a person of service. Jesus demonstrated positive influence by being a person of service.

Philippians 2:7 (KJV) says, **"...took upon him the form of a servant, and was made in the likeness of men:"**

I was inspired when I heard the story of Harry Rosen. Rosen is a successful businessman who used his influence to serve a community in Orlando, Florida. There was a 25 percent high school graduation rate in the Tangelo Park neighborhood. Harry Rosen put into action philanthropic efforts by paying daycare for the community of nearly three thousand people. High school students were offered free tuition for colleges in Florida. Now, the high school graduation rate is near One Hundred Percent. Rosen has donated close to ten million dollars to influence this community. Henry Rosen said, "Hospitality really is appreciating a fellow human being," Rosen's positive influence affected the daily lives of the Tangelo Park community. The desires of your heart flows with your effort of positive influence.

How do You Activate the Mind of Christ?

When I had the opportunity to work on a specific project in my previous career, I felt empowered. My expectation was to go further in my career. I didn't feel empowered when I returned to my position with no acknowledgment of what I accomplished. I knew then my career was not going any further. My self-worth went into the trash. I know for sure I was not living from my spirit. My confidence and self-worth took a dive because I wasn't putting into action the truth of who I am and God's plans for my life. My empowerment was in cultural norms, not God's truth. I didn't empower myself in God's truth regarding my authentic image, talent, nor influence. Isaiah 65:16 (KJV) says, **"That he who blesseth himself in the earth shall bless himself in the God of truth**; and he that sweareth in the earth shall swear by the God of truth; because the former troubles are forgotten, and because they are hid from mine eyes." The mind of Christ is activated in your life when you empower yourself in the truth of your spiritual foundation. Therefore, you must act on what Jesus appointed you to do in your authentic image, talent, and influence. You must make it a priority to live from your spirit in God's truth. This includes putting on the mind of Christ to have dominion over your human nature. The following are three steps to put on the mind of Christ:

1. Recognize

Recognize you are anointed by God to be who you were created to be and live his plans for your life. 2 Corinthians 1:21 (NIV) says, "Now it is God who makes both us and you stand firm in Christ. **He anointed us**." God anointed your mind to experience desires in your heart. Allow the anointing to affect your mind regarding how you see yourself in Christ. Recognizing that you are set apart from your weakness, failures, past, cultural norms, educational experiences, etc. This includes separating your mind from people's opinion of you, job titles, failures, past success, age, retirement, limited beliefs, etc. Overall, separate your mind from anything that opposes your authentic image, talent, and influence. Don't consider your former life when putting God's truth into action.

2. Receive

Receive the anointing by allowing the Holy Spirit to teach you. 1 John 2:27 (NIV) says, "As for you, the anointing you received from him remains in you, and you do not need anyone to teach you. But as his anointing teaches you about all things and as that anointing is real, not counterfeit—just as it has taught you, remain in him." Jesus was not a counterfeit. Jesus didn't allow deceit to come from his mouth to manipulate people. The Holy Spirit's job is to teach you how to be the authentic you, while using your talent and influence. You don't despise others success when you receive the anointing. You stay in faith when you suffer for being the person you were created to be. We are all wired differently. You were created to use your talent and influence different from others. Only the Holy Spirit can teach you how to allow the anointing to flow in skills, talents, abilities.

I had the pleasure of seeing gospel singer, Todd Dulaney, in concert. I must admit that I experienced praise and worship in a fresh way. Literally, I could feel God's presence infusing my body. Words cannot express my experience. I can tell you that it was the anointing on Todd Dulaney's image, talent, and influence that caused me to experience God's presence. He mentioned in an interview that gospel singer, Smokey Norful, mentored him in preparation for his music career. Smokey could not teach Todd on how his talent and influence should be used in the anointing. Only the Holy Spirit could teach Todd on how to be creative living the desires of his heart. They have different life experiences that only the Holy Spirit can navigate them through. The anointing on Smokey and Todd's lives are expressed differently. This is why Smokey and Todd songs are different. They're doing the work Jesus chose and appointed them for. You will be in a room with people who have the same talent as you. You will display your talent different than others when you allow the anointing to flow in your image, talent, and influence.

3. Reproduce

Reproduce your image, talent, and influence by faith in God's power. There is a wealth of information on the internet. "Google it" is a familiar phrase we hear in our time. You have the ability to get information on any subject, place, people, things, etc. through google search engine.

It's helpful when you want to locate a business or learn about things that are interesting to you. For example, I "googled" life purpose. Google reproduced about 2,840,000,000 results on life purpose in 0.56 seconds. The information I received are more likely from credible sources. The sources may provide tips that I may apply immediately in my life. Here is the truth. You can't google information to reproduce your life in Christ. You need God's power to reproduce your life. 1 Corinthians 2:5 (KJV) says, "That your faith should not stand in the wisdom of men, but in **the power of God**." God's power break barriers through the anointing. Human knowledge cannot move you beyond barriers that are clogging your heart. Human knowledge and ability are limited. God's knowledge and power are limitless. Your faith in God's power will help you put into action his knowledge to living the desires in your heart. Your commitment to God is how you consistently reproduce your image, talent, and influence.

The mind of Christ is one mindset for everyone who are followers of Jesus. This mindset releases the power of

God for everyone to be who they were created to be. This is a mindset that causes everyone to be fruitful, multiply, and replenish the earth. The purpose of this mindset is to serve one another in love. This mindset is separate from strife and selfishness. It's wrapped in humility. It's God's gift to you.

Chapter 6 Summary

- The mind of Christ is a mindset that releases God's power
- Jesus' mind was anointed by God to demonstrate God's power over human nature
- Knowledge was Jesus' method to use His mind with the full intention to give life
- Jesus received God's knowledge to live life
- **Consider the following when discovering what Jesus chose and appointed you to do:**

  1. Who you are in Christ

  2. Your talents

  3. Your influence

  4. The problems you are called to solve

- Jesus' strategy to keep a mindset of humility is to be a person of no reputation
- Jesus' strategy for using talent is obedience.
- Jesus' strategy for influence is to serve people.
- The mind of Christ is activated in your life when you empower yourself in the truth of your spiritual foundation
- The following are three steps to put on the mind of Christ:

  1. Recognize you are anointed by God to be who you were created to be and live God's plans for your life

2. Receive the anointing by allowing the Holy Spirit to teach you

3. Reproduce your image, talent, and influence by faith in God's power

A Call To Action

You were gifted with a mind equipped with intellect to be the best version of yourself. The mind of Christ is your gift to serve people in your authentic image with your talent and influence.

Recognize, receive, and reproduce the mind of Christ in your daily living. God's power is available to you when you expect it to work in your life by faith. This power is for you to experience in humility, obedience, and service. This includes renewing your mind to God's truth. Ephesians 4:23 (KJV) says, **"And be renewed in the spirit of your mind;"** This is an opportunity for you to release the new you.

Pray the following prayer:

Lord,

I recognize, receive, and choose to reproduce the mind of Christ in my daily living. My faith is in your power, not the wisdom of men. I receive your teachings, instructions, and guidance to live your plans for my life. I ask for your strength to be renewed in the spirit of my mind. I choose to renew my mind in your word. Therefore, I affirm I am a humble and obedient servant to you and the people you called me to serve. Thank you for giving me the mind of Christ to be in oneness with you.

In Jesus' Name.

Meditate
Read and meditate on Philippians 2:2-13. Remember to take time out of your day without any distractions to mediate.

Chapter 7

The Law of the Spirit of Life in Christ Jesus

"For the law of the Spirit of life in Christ Jesus hath made me free from the law of sin and death."

Romans 8:2 (KJV)

"You abandoned your spiritual life," was God response to me. I prayed after returning home from a counseling session. I asked God for instructions regarding the depression and anxiety I was experiencing. My back was against the wall when I left my counseling session.

After several sessions, my counselor asked, "what are you going to do about your situation?" I left knowing my life was going to spiral out of control if I didn't get a hold of this issue. This is the truth you must face when dealing with life issues. The truth is; God is the answer to every problem you are facing. First, I had to face the truth that I abandoned my spiritual life. There came a time in my life where everything was going well. I went from praying and meditating daily to whenever there was a need. I went from having a relationship with God to putting him in my "back pocket" when I needed him. So, I would just meet God at church. I didn't realize I was embracing a life of my own pleasures. Most important that my life of own pleasures put me on the fast track to sorrow in my heart. I lived a spiritual lifestyle for ten years. I was in rhythm with God. I recall a time when a co-worker said, "you are so peaceful." My co-worker witnessed the Law of the Spirit of Life in Christ Jesus in my life.

God was right; I abandoned my spiritual life and got in rhythm with the law of sin and death. I woke up one day depressed and anxious because I was operating under the law of sin and death. Sorrow clogged my heart. The life of God cannot flow from your heart under the law of sin and death. The Law of the Spirit of Life in Christ Jesus was established by the blood of Jesus. Ephesians 1:7 (KJV) says, **"In whom we have redemption through his blood, the forgiveness of sins, according to the riches of his grace;"** One definition for redemption is to perform what has been promised. The Law of the Spirit of Life in Christ Jesus is for you to experience your redemption of what is promised to you through the blood of Jesus. The law of the Spirit is what I would refer to the remainder of this chapter.

The law of the Spirit executes the following:

- Freedom from the law of sin and death (Romans 8:2)
- Dominion over the law of human nature and law of sin and death (Romans 8:3-4)
- Gives life because of righteousness (Romans 8:10)
- Adoption to be a child of God (Romans 8:15)
- Gives witness to your spirit that you are a child of God (Romans 8:16)
- Helps you in your weakness (Romans 8:26)
- Intercedes for you with groans; wordless expressions (Romans 8:26)
- Prays God's will for your life (Romans 8:27)

The law of the Spirit is your place of freedom. The freedom to be who you were created to be in Christ. The desires of your heart are connected to your freedom in Christ. This is God's promise to you.

God's Promises to You

Freedom in Jesus Christ is about you "being" who you are in God's image. In addition to you being saved, God-made plans for you is to think, talk, and act like him. Romans 8:29 (NIV) says, "For those God foreknew he also

predestined to be conformed to the image of his Son, that he might be the firstborn among many brothers and sisters." God predestined you to be conformed to the image of Jesus. God predestined you to live in oneness with him. Just think for a moment that God expects for you to act like Jesus. I bring this up because this is the reason God went out of his way to make sure you had the opportunity to be conformed to Jesus' image. This is one promise to you. The second promise is being adopted by God. Ephesians 1:5 (KJV) says, **"Having predestinated us unto the adoption of children by Jesus Christ to himself, according to the good pleasure of his will,"** God adopted you by Jesus to guarantee your freedom in Christ. This is good news! Every day, you see with your eyes or remember from your past the rejection or oppression you experience from people or "systems" that cause you to feel alone.

One of the greatest experiences I had was receiving my certification to be a speaker, trainer, and coach. This event was special because I experienced genuine acceptance of who I am. A place where I was free to be myself with freedom of thought and creativity. I had the opportunity to share my story, and people received me with love and appreciation. I loved this because I didn't have to hide expressing myself for fear of rejection. I was in an environment where I was celebrated for just "being" me. This is the same type of experience God planned for you when you received Jesus in your heart. God wants you to experience the freedom of belonging to him. He celebrates you for who you are.

Zephaniah 3:17 (KJV) says, "The LORD thy God in the midst of thee is mighty; he will save, he will rejoice over thee with joy; he will rest in his love, he will joy over thee with singing." God made sure that you are empowered to be like Jesus by adopting you as his child. You are a child of God. This is a truth that God takes pleasure in according to his will for your life. This is not according to a church membership, family, race, gender, or political party. This stands on you receiving the truth of who you are in Christ.

You may be asking, "Why am I experiencing weaknesses, failures, drama, or disappointment in my life while being in God's family?" You experience desires in your heart when you are intentional about living God's will for your life. **You may say,** "I tried it, and it didn't work." **I ask you with a smile,** "Did you allow the Holy Spirit to guide you into all truth?" This brings up the third promise, which is the promise of the Spirit. Galatians 3:14 (NIV) says, "He redeemed us in order that the blessing given to Abraham might come to the Gentiles **through Christ**

Jesus, so that by faith we might receive the promise of the Spirit." The promise of the Spirit is God's promise to assist you in being who you were created to be while living his plans for your life. In other words, assist you in discovering and living the desires of your heart. The Holy Spirit, your promise from God, is your Helper, Comforter, Counselor, Intercessor, Advocate, and Standby (ready to assist with power).

There is a "why" to everything God does. God certified you as his own by giving you the Holy Spirit in your heart. 2 Corinthians 1:22 (KJV) says, "Who hath also sealed us, and given the earnest of the Spirit in our hearts." The Holy Spirit is your deposit that guarantees your inheritance as a child of God. Why do you need the Holy Spirit? The following is why the Holy Spirit is here for you:

- To Help (Romans 8:26)
- To Guide (John 16:13)
- To Teach (1 John 2:27)
- To Reveal (1 Corinthians 2:10)
- To Empower (Acts 1:8)
- To Quicken Your Spirit; Make Alive (John 6:63)

There are more than three promises God has for you. The promise of being conformed into God's image, adopted as a child of God, and the promise of the Spirit operates under the **Law of the Spirit of Life in Christ Jesus.**

The law of the Spirit recognizes the "New You." I challenge you by faith to engage your newness of life. Romans 6:4 (KJV) says, "Therefore we are buried with him by baptism into death: that like as Christ was raised up from the dead by the glory of the Father, **even so, we also should walk in newness of life**." God empowered you with promises to live your new life. Therefore, you must be intentional with the mind of Christ to live your "New Life" under the law of the Spirit.

Your Faith

God created the universe by faith. You were made in his image and likeness to live the desires of your heart by faith. The law of the Spirit is activated by your faith and functions in God's truth.

While you are embracing the truths in this book, the fact remains that you are dealing with life circumstances that are connected to your five senses of hearing, sight, touch, smell, and taste. Your physical body can relate to what you have experienced throughout your life. You may have a family background, dependence on any type of substance, credit score, bank account, divorce, relationship, etc. that are opposite of your newness of life. You wake up each day knowing what God placed in your heart, but your life circumstance causes you to accept life as it is. Your mind has adapted to your life experiences.

You base your thinking on the tradition from what you have experienced. Your five senses are connected to thoughts driven by tradition from experiences. I was limited to this type of thinking. It took me eighteen months to detox my mind from thinking according to tradition. My mindset was limited to thinking the way I was conditioned in my mind. This was a danger zone for me because I spent eighteen years at a job that didn't allow freedom of expression, creativity, critical thinking, etc. Everything was driven by policy and procedures. This created limited-thinking full of tradition. I conformed to the worker they expected of me in my career and personal life. This caused me to ignore the desires hidden in my heart. Overall, I denied my right to experience newness of life.

This is a danger zone because your heart can become blinded to the truth of who you are and God's plans for your life. The law of the Spirit operates in God's truth. His word has final authority under the law of the Spirit. This means thinking connected tradition and experiences has no place under the law of the Spirit.

What I didn't realize after I ended my career that my heart was far from God. My self-worth was measured based on my career. My mind was attached to the job title, duties, and salary. My life was centered on giving my all in my career. This was a tradition that I held in my heart. The truth is I had more faith in my employer promoting me than God.

Jesus addressed tradition with the Pharisees when they found fault with the disciples eating food without washing their hands. They held the tradition of the elders to hold a ceremony of washing hands before they eat. The Pharisees and teachers of the law asked Jesus in Mark 7:5 (NIV), "Why don't your disciples live according to the tradition of the elders instead of eating their food with defiled hands?" Jesus recognized where their hearts were. He let the Pharisees and teacher of the law know that their hearts were far from him. Jesus said in Mark 7:8 (NIV), "You have let go of the commands of God and are holding on to human traditions." Marks 7:13 (NIV) says, "Thus you nullify the word of God by your tradition that you have handed down. And you do many things like that." Tradition stops God's word from working in your life. What traditions do you hold in your heart that are contrary to God's word? Tradition may be from your career, family, affiliation with organizations, education, etc. Jesus emphasized this with the disciples.

In Mark 7:20-21 (NIV), Jesus said, "What comes out of a person is what defiles them. [21] For it is from within, out of a person's heart,..." Any tradition you hold in your heart is what defiles your divine nature in God. I had to look at every area of my life when traditions came before me. I'm bringing this up because your traditions will be assessed by God. Your faith in God's word is what will keep you moving forward beyond tradition in your newness of life. Newness of life is "becoming" who you are in Christ. This is where you need faith and a spiritual mind to experience the desires in your heart. This calls for new thinking, new imagination, new will, new memory, new ways, new emotions, new attitude, new ideas, new plans, etc. Faith is required to use your spiritual mind, which allows the law of the Spirit to move you beyond life circumstances. The battle takes place in your mind.

Your Spiritual Mind

There is a war that takes place in your mind when you are discovering and living the desires of your heart. This is not a one-time event. This is where you fight to have dominion over your life. REMEMBER, THIS IS DONE BY FAITH.

This fight calls for being single-minded while being intentional and focused to live in your newness of life. The single-mind is being spiritually minded. A spiritually minded person recognizes God is their source for their "state of being." They recognize their source to life comes from their spirit. The word of God is the final authority in their life. They use their perception, imagination, intuition, reason, memory, and will according to God's word. The results they get under the law of the Spirit is life and peace.

A carnal mind is opposite of the spiritual mind. A carnal mind may have accepted Jesus but have not fully followed God with their heart. Their mind is driven by what they see, smell, touch, hear, and taste. Their decisions are made on tradition and experiences. Their life is consumed with pleasures. I had a carnal mind which led to depression, anxiety, fears, and worries, etc. A carnal mind's perception, imagination, intuition, reason, memory, and will are separate from God. Romans 8:6 (KJV) says, "For to be carnally minded is death; but to be spiritually minded is life and peace." The mind of Christ is the spiritual mind that gives you the power to live a spiritual lifestyle.

Here is a comparison of a carnal mind and spiritual mind

Carnal Mind	Spiritual Mind In Christ
Trusts Intellect	Trusts God
Dreads Life	Desires Life
Lacks Patience	Patient
In a Hurry	Remains Calm
Agitated Mind	Peaceful Mind
Driven by Emotions	Driven by the Holy Spirit

You have to identify which mindset you need to discover and live the desires of your heart. My intention is to encourage you so that you experience all desires in your heart. This is a road you must travel to identify the type of mindset to use when you commit to God's plans for your life.

I believe followers of Christ love God. The challenge they experience the most is being double-minded. A double-minded person uses a carnal and spiritual mind. A double-minded person wavers in faith. One morning, they put on a spiritual mind. Before noon, they choose a carnal mind because they are doubting God's ability in a situation they are facing. James 1:8 (NIV) says, "Such a person is double-minded and unstable in all they do."

Everyone has desires hidden in their heart. There's a time when a person pursues the desires. Let's use dieting as an example. A person makes the decision to go on a diet. They start eating the right foods, but they eat cookies in the evening due to stress. They encountered a situation they dreaded and responded by indulging in cookies. Dread showed up in their life. Negative emotions trigger them to respond and ignore their desire to lose weight.

"I'm guilty, been there and done that." A double mind creates instability. My mentor, Paul Martinelli, says, "How you do anything is how you do everything." He is right. This is the war that takes place in your mind. Romans 7:23 (KJV) says, "But I see another law in my members, warring against the law of my mind, and bringing me into captivity to the law of sin which is in my members." Dread is under the law of sin and death.

Dread connects to circumstances you perceive are bigger than you. This causes you to believe you are stuck. One definition of dread is great fear or apprehension. A person looks at their circumstances and shrink back when God ask them to do something.

Here is an illustration when God asks people to do something

God's Desire	A Person's Response
Start a Business	I'm scared of the risk involved
Work on an invention	I don't have the time
Create Jewelry	There aren't enough opportunities
Open a Restaurant	I fear my family disapproval
Change Careers	I am content with where I am

People will live their entire life with dread in their mind. Dread will cause you to hesitate from pursuing the desires in your heart. At the same time, dread will cause you to think that your life is fine. Dread grows in:

- Low self-esteem: Thoughts of being unworthy of experiencing more in life

- Comfort zones: Comfort zones put a cap on your potential

- Complacency: Complacency kills dreams

- Indifference: Live life as it is, which creates an attitude of "I don't care, either way"

I must be honest with you. As I'm writing this chapter, dread showed up this morning, asking, "Who will read my book?" My answer is people whose lives will be transformed by this book. This is why I ignored the thought and kept writing. My desire is that everyone who reads this book lives will experience transformation through God's word. What has God asked you to do? Do you immediately look at a part of your life that you dread? Deuteronomy 1:29

(KJV) says, "Then I said unto you, Dread not, neither be afraid of them." The answer to handling dread is to use your spiritual mind, moving forward.

Take Action

A spiritual mind creates stability in your life. You are able to be intentional in discovering and living the desires of your heart. Your newness in life. Desires vibrates to God's word under the Law of the Spirit. You can look at a situation that is full of people's criticism of you and move forward without their validation. This gives you the ability to focus on what God has placed in your heart. This happens when you take action to be spiritually minded.

A spiritual mindset involves taking action to live in your freedom while focusing on the things in the spirit. Romans 8:5 (KJV) says, "For they that are after the flesh do mind the things of the flesh; but they that are after the Spirit the things of the Spirit." Your freedom is to live from your spirit in the newness of life. The purpose is to serve others with love.

Galatians 5:13-14 (NIV) says, "You, my brothers and sisters, were called to be free. But do not use your freedom to indulge the flesh; rather, serve one another humbly in love. [14] For the entire law is fulfilled in keeping this one command: 'Love your neighbor as yourself.'" Love allows you to live in the newness of your life. This is the place where you experience your oneness and divine nature in God. This is a place of battle in the mind.

While getting clarity about desires in my heart, I was challenged to be offended by certain individuals. There was a time I received a life-changing word from God. I interacted with a particular person who intentionally used me regarding an issue. I recognized after they left my presence how they intentionally used me. I rehearsed the issue in my mind all day. Dread was creeping, taking my focus off my desires to be nurtured in my mind. The Holy Spirit put me in remembrance to let it go. My inner witness said, "Are you going to exalt me or yourself in the situation?" Immediately, I let it go and began praying that the offensive be removed from me.

I made the decision to forgive the person and didn't discuss it anymore. My spiritual mind was in operation. This is an example of producing the fruit of the Spirit, which are results of God's power working in your life. A spiritual mind bears the fruit of the spirit, confirmed in Galatians Chapter 5. Galatians 5:22-23 (NIV) says, "But the fruit of the

Spirit is love, joy, peace, forbearance, kindness, goodness, faithfulness, [23] gentleness, and self-control. Against such things, there is no law." This is the fruit in your life that Jesus chose and appointed you to produce. You soar into experiencing your authentic image, talent, and influence when you use love to be spiritually minded in Christ. This includes displaying the fruit of the Spirit:

1. Love: Expressed love for God, self, and people
2. Joy: Excitement of the mind expressing happiness of God's goodness
3. Peace: Quietness of mind – consistently being in a calm state
4. Forbearance: Displaying habits of patience without complaining
5. Kindness: Contribute to the happiness of others – includes being respectful
6. Goodness: Acts of compassion and mercy
7. Faithfulness: Loyal to commitments and consistent in positive actions with people
8. Gentleness: Mild manners with a gentle temper
9. Self-Control: Ability to control thinking, emotions, and behaviors

There is one step that you must make to be spiritually minded, which is the following:

1. Don't Condemn Yourself

During this week of writing this chapter, I frustrated the grace of God. Galatians 2:21 (KJV) says, "I do not frustrate the grace of God: for if righteousness come by the law, then Christ is dead in vain." I made a decision without seeking God's advice. I was convicted in my heart. Immediately, I repented to God, but I felt condemned. I must admit, I didn't feel worthy to finish the book. Romans 8:1 (KJV), "There is therefore now no condemnation to them which are in Christ Jesus, who walk not after the flesh, but after the Spirit." Jesus paid the price for my mistake. Jesus sacrificed his life so you can be spiritually minded. You are worthy. Guilt and shame have no place in your heart. Therefore, don't judge yourself regarding your sins, failures, past, disappointments, etc. It is under the blood of Jesus. Instead, be quick to repent then get up and move forward, being spiritually minded. 1 John 1:9 (KJV) says, "If we confess our sins, he is faithful and just to forgive us our sins, and to cleanse us from all unrighteousness." Enjoy your freedom to be who you were created to be in Christ!

Chapter 7 Summary

- The Law of the Spirit of Life in Christ Jesus was established by the blood of Jesus
- The Law of the Spirit of Life in Christ Jesus is for you to experience your redemption of what is promised to you through the blood of Jesus
- **The law of the Spirit executes the following:**
  1. Freedom from the law of sin and death (Romans 8:2)
  2. Dominion over the law of human nature and law of sin and death (Romans 8:3-4)
  3. Gives life because of righteousness (Romans 8:10)
  4. Adoption to be a child of God (Romans 8:15)
  5. Gives witness to your spirit that you are a child of God (Romans 8:16)
  6. Helps you in your weakness (Romans 8:26)
  7. Intercedes for you with groans; wordless expressions (Romans 8:26)
  8. Prays God's will for your life (Romans 8:27)
- God predestined you to be conformed to the image of Jesus
- God adopted you by Jesus to guarantee your freedom in Christ

- The promise of the Spirit is God's promise to assist you in being who you were created to be while living God's plans for your life
- **The Holy Spirit helps you:**
  1. To Help (Romans 8:26)
  2. To Guide (John 16:13)
  3. To Teach (1 John 2:27)
  4. To Reveal (1 Corinthians 2:10)
  5. To Empower (Acts 1:8)
  6. To Quicken Your Spirit; Make Alive (John 6:63)
- The law of the Spirit is activated by your faith and functions in God's truth
- A spiritually minded person recognizes God is their source for their "state of being"
- A spiritual mindset involves taking action to live in your freedom, while focusing on the things in the spirit
- **Don't Condemn Yourself:** Don't judge yourself regarding your sins, failures, past, disappointments, etc. It is under the blood of Jesus

A Call To Action

Jesus set you free from the law of sin and death. Jesus made the Law of the Spirit of Life in Christ Jesus available to you by his blood. The blood of Jesus covers every area of your life.

You have the right to affirm the blood of Jesus over yourself, spouse, children, home, career, car, circumstances, etc., under the Law of the Spirit of Life in Christ Jesus. This is your place of refuge in God. Therefore, it's important to be spiritually-minded through a spiritual lifestyle. Romans 8:6 (KJV) says, "For to be carnally minded is death; but to be spiritually minded is life and peace." Life and peace are your gateway to living the desires of your heart.

Pray the following prayer:

Lord,

I desire for your word to engrave my mind, imagination, memory, perception, reason, intuition, and will. The entrance of your word is light in my life. Your word is the path that takes me higher in thinking and taking action in my daily living. Romans 8:39 (NIV) says, **"neither height nor depth, nor anything else in all creation, will be able to separate us from the love of God that is in Christ Jesus our Lord."** I affirm nothing can separate me from your love that is found in Jesus. I am more than a conqueror. Thank you for allowing me to live under the Law of the Spirit of Life in Christ Jesus.

In Jesus Name.

Meditate

Read and meditate on Romans Chapter 8

Chapter 8

Grow in Wisdom

"But grow in grace, and in the knowledge of our Lord and Saviour Jesus Christ. To him be glory both now and for ever. Amen."

2 Peter 3:18 (KJV)

I will never forget May 25, 2014. This was the day I came into the awareness that God needed me just as much as I needed him. I walked out of Lakewood Church in Houston, Texas, free. I left behind the weight of dread on my life. I was ready to take on the world. I knew God had an assignment for me, but I didn't know what it was.

I knew the guest speaker Bishop TD Jakes' message was my divine appointment with my new beginning with God. I returned home ready to take on the world. There was a newness about me. I was definitely "woke" regarding my freedom in Christ, but depression returned in 2015. I was "woke" and still broken. My spiritual foundation continued to leak. What happened? I heard the word but didn't take action. I thought I was moving forward after receiving the message. James 1:22 (KJV) says, **"But be ye doers of the word, and not hearers only, deceiving your own selves."** I deceived myself. I was not living a spiritual lifestyle. I was just going to church. I heard the word with no action. Every follower of Christ must put God's word into action to discover and live desires in their heart.

There are three types of people reading this book. They are the following:

1. People who receive God's truth and will put into practice
2. People who will be awakened to God's truth but will not put it into practice
3. People who will reject God's truth

The key to experiencing God's truth is putting it into practice. Your conscious becomes aware of where you're at in your life. It's like a carbon-monoxide detector. Your conscious helps you identify areas in your life that are suffocating you. This is during a time when God is touching your heart. Hebrews 3:15 (KJV) says, "While it is said, To day if ye will hear his voice, harden not your hearts, as in the provocation." God wants you to turn your desire towards him with your heart. This is why God asked Adam, "where are you?" Your conscious becomes aware of God tugging on your heart. Your conscious makes the following remarks:

"I need to pray more."

"I need to read my Bible more."

"I need to forgive."

This is how God nudges you to put his truth into action. Truth is rejected when it's not acknowledged with faith and action. This is where delusion kicks in.

I heard Bishop Jakes' message, but I was delusional, thinking I was okay while I remained in the cycle of depression. Delusion is **a form of deception; a misleading of the mind.** I remained delusional in my perception, imagination, intuition, reasoning, memory, and will. 2 Thessalonians 2:11-12 (KJV) says, "And for this cause God shall send them strong delusion, that they should believe a lie: [12] That they all might be damned who believed not the truth, but had pleasure in unrighteousness." Every day, you are faced with the decision to believe the truth of who you were created to be or believe the lie.

God truth is connected to your authentic image, talent, influence, and plans for your life. I didn't take ownership of my truth after I heard Bishop Jakes' message. I went home, continuing to live the cycle of pleasure. I continued to lack sound judgment connected to decisions that caused depression in my life. I was sharing with a close friend on the phone the discomfort I was experiencing from depression. Her response to me was, "you have the word, use your authority."

My conscious made me aware that I needed to turn my desire towards God. This was when I followed step one in this book. I rested in God. I committed to step two by allowing the mind of Christ to expand in my mind. Step 3, I made the sacrifice to grow in wisdom. 1 Peter 2:2 (KJV) says, "As newborn babes, desire the sincere milk of the word, that ye may grow thereby:" I desired to grow in God's word. God's word is wisdom. Desires of the heart include the desire to grow in God's word. Growth is a spiritual lifestyle in Christ.

A spiritual lifestyle in Christ is having the discipline to live by the word of God. In Luke 4:4 (KJV), Jesus said, **"It is written, that man shall not live by bread alone, but by every word of God."** Spiritual growth is required to develop the discipline to live by God's word. Discovering and living the desires of your heart is a process. The process includes spiritual growth. Spiritual growth is developing the discipline to grow in wisdom. Jesus grew in wisdom. Luke 2:52 (NIV) says, "And **Jesus grew in wisdom and stature**, and in favor with God and man." By law, no person has the ability to conform to the image of Jesus without spiritual growth in Christ

You are the Church

Do you ever wonder where the church is when you see problems in the world? I remember sitting in my office at the school when I was burdened with the issues students experience. Every day, I was overwhelmed with witnessing students being homeless, prostituting, suffering from assaults, looking for food, etc. I asked God, "Where is the church?" God responded, "You are the church." I shared this story to share the following message to you: **You are the church! God needs you to be a solution the world needs.**

1 Peter 2:5 (KJV) says, "Ye also, as lively stones, are built up a spiritual house, an holy priesthood, to offer up spiritual sacrifices, acceptable to God by Jesus Christ." A spiritual house is built by growing in wisdom. You expand and progress your mind in wisdom. This is why God made

you in his divine nature to be the church. You are the solution to someone's problem. This is why it's important to be a spiritual house to live from the spiritual foundation of your authentic image, talent, and influence. It is a sacrifice to be a spiritual house.

Growth doesn't occur without a sacrifice. Romans 12:1 (KJV) says, "I beseech you therefore, brethren, by the mercies of God, that ye present your bodies a living sacrifice, holy, acceptable unto God, which is your reasonable service." Allowing your life to be governed by God's word is a sacrifice. You sacrifice your plans for God's plans for your life. You give up your ways for God's ways on how you handle life matters. Dale and I agreed to have a two-person household before we were married. Things changed when I knew God was calling me into personal growth. Dale made the sacrifice to carry the financial weight when he agreed that I could resign from my career. This was a financial sacrifice for our household. This was a sacrifice for me to grow in wisdom. Wisdom offers instruction and knowledge before experiencing the desires in your heart. Proverbs 8:10 (KJV) says,

"Receive my instruction, and not silver; and knowledge rather than choice gold." Sacrifice comes with wisdom instructions. You sacrifice your thoughts for God's thoughts. Allowing God's will to be your destiny is a sacrifice. This is the sacrifice to live in your oneness with God. This comes with growing in wisdom.

Build Your Spiritual House

In Chapter 1 (Desires of the Heart), I gave an illustration on how desires are seeking to flow into your life the same way water seeps through the foundation of a house. A spiritual house is needed for desires to flow from your heart.

Building a spiritual house requires a spiritual foundation. A foundation is the basis or groundwork on which anything stands. Jesus left the blueprint on how to build your spiritual house. Jesus acknowledged that your spiritual foundation is laid by putting his teachings into practice. Jesus said in Luke 6:47- 48 (NIV), "As for everyone who comes to me and hears my words and puts them into practice, I will show you what they are like. [48] They are like a man building a house, who dug down deep and laid the foundation on rock. When a flood came, the torrent struck that house but could not shake it, because it was well built." God's word is the foundation to build your spiritual house. This is the foundation for you to grow in wisdom.

Your spiritual house holds the light energy that flows from your heart. 2 Corinthians 4:6 (KJV) says, "For God, who commanded the light to shine out of darkness, hath shined in our hearts, to give the light of the knowledge of the glory of God in the face of Jesus Christ." Jesus shines in your heart. 2 Peter 1:19 (NIV) says, "We also have the prophetic message as something completely reliable, and you will do well to pay attention to it, as to a light shining in a dark place, until the day dawns and the morning star rises in your hearts." Jesus is the morning star that rises in your heart. Revelations 22:16 (KJV) says, "I, Jesus, have sent mine angel to testify unto you these things in the churches. I am the root and the offspring of David, and the bright and morning star." This is your power to productivity. You have the power to produce the fruit Jesus chose and appointed you to produce.

The power to the foundation of your desire:

1. To be who God created you to be in Christ
2. Live God's plans for your life

This light is your source for living. This is the light that God spoke into the earth. Genesis 1:3 (KJV) says, "And God said, Let there be light: and there was light."
This light is fluid, which means it easily flows without separation. This means light flows into different parts of God's creation, independent of other substances.
The following are the descriptions of light:

God	1 John 1:15
God's Word	Psalm 119:105
Jesus	John 8:12
Life	John 1:4
You are the light of the world	Matthew 5:14
Light given to the mind for understanding	Ephesians 1:18

This is why Jesus said he acknowledges people who put his teachings into action. The light energy force of God expands in your life when you get knowledge from God's word. Therefore, your spiritual house is built with your conscience.

Your conscious allows you to know yourself while your conscience gives you internal knowledge to put God's word into action. Knowledge is putting truth into action. educo is the Latin root word for educate, which means to draw out. Your conscience allows you to draw out your knowledge of God's word when you need it.

For example, I was waiting for cars to pass in the left turn lane before proceeding to turn. The car behind me aggressively honked their horn, implying I should turn immediately. It was clear that I couldn't turn without being in an accident. They kept honking the horn as I waited patiently to turn. I was tempted to get agitated and respond while I waited, but my conscience was telling me to ignore them. Peace came over me as I made the decision to ignore them. Your conscience is where God puts his laws for you to live the desires of the heart. Hebrews 10:16 (KJV) says, "This is the covenant that I will make with them after those days, saith the Lord, **I will put my laws into their hearts, and in their minds will I write them**;" Your conscience is a part of your mind that gives you the ability to draw out God's knowledge as you need it.

Your conscience knows the truth of God's word, which is confirmed by the Holy Spirit. Romans 9:1 (NIV) says, **"I speak the truth in Christ—I am not lying, my conscience confirms it through the Holy Spirit-"** Your conscience is the voice of your human spirit. This is the inward witness of your spirit. Jesus purged your conscience to live a life he chose you to produce. Hebrews 9:14 (KJV) says, "How much more shall the blood of Christ, who through the eternal Spirit offered himself without spot to God, **purge your conscience from dead works to serve the living God?"** The knowledge your conscience draws out to build your spiritual house is wisdom.

What does it take to build a spiritual home? It takes being a standout to build a spiritual house for God. A standout is a person who hears from God and receives his teachings and instructions. Jesus said in John 6:45 (NIV), "It is written in the Prophets: 'They will all be taught by God.' **Everyone who has heard the Father and learned from him comes to me."**

A chameleon is a person who seeks God's word but wavers in their faith. They have a double mind to follow God's way one day, but on a different day, they make choices opposite of God's thoughts and ways. A chameleon is unable to keep the commitment to build a spiritual house. James 1:8 (KJV), "**A double-minded man is unstable in all his ways.**" A chameleon has a double mind towards God.

A sore thumb is a person who does not fear God and rejects his knowledge. Proverbs 1:29-30 (KJV) says, "**For that they hated knowledge,** and did not choose the fear of the LORD: [30] They would none of my counsel: they despised all my reproof."

The following is a comparison of a standout, chameleon, and sore thumb.

Standout	Chameleon	Sore Thumb
•Increase in learing •Motivated by love •Study to be quiet •Focus on their own life •Peaceable •Merciful to people •Avoid hypocrisy •Use their talent & influence	•Stop learning •Live by cultural trends •Distracted •Drift in thinking •Express limited love towards people •Use God as a "get out of jail card"	•Seek pleasure •Question God's nature •Debate issues •Confused •Promote strife •Entertain certain people life issues •Untamed tongue •Depend on five senses

I illustrated the comparison to encourage you to identify your areas of growth. I honestly tell you; I was a chameleon and sore thumb at different times in life.

I had to strategically identify areas of growth. Please don't take yourself into self-judgment. Growth comes with birthing the new you. The birthing of a newborn is messy. A new creation comes from a messy birth. I challenge you to consider the following areas to grow in wisdom:

- Environment: Identify the environment that will promote your growth

- People: Identify people that will celebrate you and grow with you

- Mentors: Identify mentors who are mastering spiritual growth

- Books: In addition to reading the Bible, identify books to read, aligned with God's word

Get Wisdom

I sat at the table mentally drained after I completed an e-book titled, *Living Your Purpose*. I knew at that moment that I couldn't go further. I tried everything I thought would work in building a business. Nothing was working. I failed in every plan I attempted to put into action.

This was one of many tests from God. The only thing that mattered to me in this moment of failure was God. I was resting in God. I was operating in the mind of Christ. I needed to hear from God. I prayed and listened to two different teachings on wisdom. My mind was enlightened to know that I was lacking wisdom in my life. I needed to grow spiritually in wisdom. Proverbs 24:3-4 KJV says, "Through wisdom is an house builded; and by understanding it is established: 4 And by knowledge shall the chambers be filled with all precious and pleasant riches."

I was gaining knowledge regarding life principles, but I didn't know how to draw out desires hidden in my heart. This created friction between my spiritual and human nature. Wisdom is the right way to exercise knowledge for every area of your life. I was putting the cart before the horse. Wisdom comes before knowledge. Desires in the heart are connected to spiritual growth.

Wisdom is the key to spiritual growth. I am referring to the wisdom that comes from God. You and I may have the same problem. God's wisdom will give us two different ways to handle the problem. God's wisdom is tailored to your personal situation. Wisdom takes you from your intuition to discernment. You are able to discern the right way to use knowledge for your life.

Wisdom comes from a relationship with God. Jesus was made unto us wisdom.

1 Corinthians 1:30 (KJV) says, "But of him are ye in Christ Jesus, who of God is made unto us wisdom, and righteousness, and sanctification, and redemption:" The word of God is wisdom. You are receiving wisdom each time you read and/or meditate on God's word. God expects you to get wisdom. Proverbs 4:7 (KJV) says, "Wisdom is the principal thing; therefore get wisdom: and with all thy getting get understanding."

You are a spiritual being with intelligence. Your talent is a skill that comes with understanding. My uncle has the skill of a carpenter. He has an understanding of the foundation and frame of homes. He knows the ins and outs of building and repairing a home.

My uncle's knowledge of carpentry came from a desire to work on homes. He didn't attend a trade school. His skill expanded while being mentored by people who were skilled in carpentry. This is an example of talent with spiritual intelligence.

God has given you intellect that comes from your spirit. Wisdom is the head of your intelligence. It's the source to you getting the knowledge to expand in your authentic image, talent, and influence. This comes by growing in wisdom. Literally, Jesus who is wisdom is the carpenter of your spiritual house. Wisdom has a voice that cries to speak into your life. Proverbs 1:20 (KJV) says, "Wisdom crieth without; she uttereth her voice in the streets:" Wisdom is seeking to give you instructions and knowledge. Proverbs chapter 8 confirms wisdom's characteristics.

The following are some of the benefits of getting wisdom:

Knowledge of Inventions	Proverbs 8:12
Counsel with Understanding & Strength	Proverbs 8:14
Preserve Your Life	Proverbs 4:6
Promotion	Proverbs 4:8

Inherit Wealth & Riches	Proverbs 8:21
Discover Your Life & Obtain God's Favor	Proverbs 8:35

The starting point for you receiving wisdom is having reverence and esteem for God's divine nature. This called the fear of the Lord. Proverbs 9:10 (KJV) says, **"The fear of the LORD is the beginning of wisdom: and the knowledge of the holy is understanding."**
The fear of the Lord creates harmony between you and God. Wisdom flows with you being in harmony with God.

The following are four truths that include the fear of the Lord:

1. To hate evil, which produces injustice
2. To hate pride, which produces conceit of self
3. To hate arrogance, which produces an attitude of self-importance with an offensive and overbearing attitude. This includes taking on life matters without God and support from people.

4. To hate speaking words opposite of the truth of God's Word

"The fear of the Lord is to hate evil: pride, and arrogancy, and the evil way, and the froward mouth, do I hate." Proverbs 8:13 (KJV)

God's desire is to source you with living a full and complete life. God is not withholding anything from you based on your race, gender, family background, age, failures, etc. God does not give preference to people. God gives preference to his laws. He grants abundant life and favor to people who put his laws into action. Therefore, God grants wisdom to people who ask him. Wisdom comes when you ask God. James 1:5 (KJV) says, "If any of you lack wisdom, let him ask of God, that giveth to all men liberally, and upbraideth not; and it shall be given him." God will give you wisdom freely when you ask him.

Wisdom will come with God's instructions. It gives life to the knowledge you need to live the desires of your heart. I recently declined an opportunity that appeared to be in my best interest. I didn't want to move ahead of God. I asked God for wisdom regarding the opportunity.

I pondered the opportunity for several days. I meditated on God's word on a Saturday morning. God gave instructions for me to decline the opportunity. He gave me additional instructions on how I should move forward without the opportunity. This is an example of how God's wisdom will instruct you on how to live the desires of your heart. This creates spiritual growth and expands your knowledge on how to put God's word into action.

The following are seven truths to identify if you are growing in wisdom from God:

1. Having a spirit with a pure conscience
2. Peace without strife or debate towards people
3. Gentle in communication towards people
4. Reasonable by being considerate and listening to people
5. Having compassion for people
6. Treating people with dignity and honor
7. A life absent of deceit and false appearance

"But the wisdom that is from above is first pure, then peaceable, gentle, and easy to be entreated, full of mercy and good fruits, without partiality, and without hypocrisy."
James 3:17 (KJV)

Guard Your Heart

I couldn't wait until I got to my car to cry. I sat with my former Director for an hour after I asked her to mentor me. I shared with her my desire to be mentored. I was seeking change in my career and admired her strengths. She simply said, "No." It was a meeting of humiliation and rejection. I didn't feel empowered when I left her office. I kept the burning desire in my heart to be mentored.

One year later, I discovered the John Maxwell Team on the internet. This matched my desire to be mentored in the area of personal growth. This desire was connected to God's plans for my life. I didn't know it at the time. I needed to grow in wisdom to get God instructions regarding who would be my mentor. It was never meant for my former Director to mentor me. I thank God that I guarded my heart by keeping this desire in my heart. This is why it's important to guard your heart. Proverbs 4:23 (KJV) says, "Keep thy heart with all diligence; for out of it are the issues of life."

Guarding my heart included growing in God's wisdom to match my thoughts with God's thoughts. This is the same for you. Growth is a process that includes transforming your mind. Desires in your heart calls for you to expand beyond your current relationships, career, business, health, finances, etc. The large place that God wants to take you to requires renewing your mind. Your heart is guarded by God's word when you renew your mind daily. This separates you from perceptions, imaginations, memories, people, systems, etc. that no longer serve you.

Your heart is the portal for desires to flow. God's joy is your strength to draw out desires from your heart. Isaiah 12:3 (KJV) says, "Therefore with joy shall ye draw water out of the wells of salvation." It's important to guard your heart with joy because this is your strength to experience God's salvation in your life. Nehemiah 8:10 (KJV) says, "...for this day is holy unto our LORD: neither be ye sorry; for the joy of the LORD is your strength." Joy is satisfaction in your mind.

Negative emotions dominated my day. I smiled during the day. Sometimes, laughed and shared enjoyable moments with people. The truth remained I dreaded certain areas in my life. Hidden under my smiles and laughs was sorrow. Sorrow caused negative emotions to go into autopilot in my life. You cannot grow in God's wisdom when negative emotions are dominating your day. Negative emotions drain your energy to pursue what God placed in your heart. The truth is your spirit is fighting for territory to experience desires in your heart. The solution to this is joy. I thank God I got my joy back.

The joy of the Lord empowers you to nurture positive emotions into daily habits. Everything you do is a result of your habits. God's Joy will break the bondage of negative emotions and give you the strength to nurture positive emotions into daily habits. Joy comes from God.

What negative emotions dominate your day?

God will clothe your mind with joy when you take satisfaction in the following:

1. Take satisfaction in God (Psalm 37:4)
2. Take satisfaction in who he created you to be (Genesis 1:27)
3. Take satisfaction in your talent (2 Timothy 1:6)
4. Take satisfaction in connecting with people (Philippians 2:2)
5. Take satisfaction in God's plans for your life. (Jeremiah 29:11)

"The joy of the Lord empowers you to nurture positive emotions into daily habits. Everything you do is a result of your habits."

I challenge you to guard your heart by renewing your mind to God's truth. Meditate and speak God's word over your life. This will keep you on the path to living the desires of your heart as you grow in wisdom. Let God's joy be your strength. The action step to grow in God's wisdom is to do the following:

Love God

Loving God with your whole desire puts you in close proximity to experience desires in your heart. Love towards God is not a feeling. It is the ultimate sacrifice you make by giving him your mind, will, and emotions. God guarantees that your life will be rewarded when you seek him with all of your heart and your whole desire. This is love. There are three truths to maintain your love towards God. They are the following:

1. Worship God

One definition of worship is to honor with extravagant love and extreme submission. John 4:24 (KJV) says, **"God is a Spirit: and they that worship him must**

worship him in spirit and in truth." God breath fills your lungs. Your life literally depends on God.

One of the greatest acts of sacrifice God made was to give Jesus to the world. God sacrificed Jesus to give you his name and divine nature for you to live the desire you craved to experience your entire life. Every day, you wake up looking for your place of significance in life. This place of significance is your spiritual nature. Your worship towards God in spirit and truth releases the life of God to satisfy you with the desires of your heart.

2. Connect with a Local Church

We live in a time when going to church isn't popular. I challenge to find a pastor that will give Biblical teaching to grow spiritually. Jeremiah 3:15 (KJV) says, **"And I will give you pastors according to mine heart, which shall feed you with knowledge and understanding."** Ask God to show you the church you should join. God desires for you to connect with a local church.

3. Keep Your Mind Excited to Study God's Word

Desires of the heart come with being intentional study God's word. I challenge you to commit to studying

God's word daily. This includes practicing the presence of God. The key to knowing God's word for your life is having a mind ready to study it. Desires vibrate to God's word. The more you know about God's word, the more you expand your mind to experience desires in your heart. Acts 17:11 (KJV) says, "These were more noble than those in Thessalonica, in that they received the word with all readiness of mind, and searched the scriptures daily, whether those things were so."

Your love for God is the focus you must keep to discover and live the desires in your heart. Where your focus goes, your energy flows. God will release rivers of living water when you love and seek him with all your heart and whole desire.

Chapter 8 Summary

- The key to experiencing God's truth is putting it into practice
- Truth is rejected when it's not acknowledged with faith and put into action
- A spiritual lifestyle in Christ is having the discipline to live by the word of God
- Spiritual growth is developing the discipline to grow in wisdom
- By law, no person has the ability to conform to the image of Jesus without spiritual growth in Christ
- Growth comes with sacrifice
- Sacrifice is the price you pay for desires to flow from your heart
- A spiritual house is needed for desires to flow from your heart
- Your conscience is the voice of your human spirit
- Wisdom is the key to spiritual growth
- The starting point for you receiving wisdom is having reverence and esteem for God's divine nature
- Wisdom comes when you ask God
- Your heart is guarded by God's word when you renew your mind daily
- It's important to guard your heart with joy because this is your strength to experience God's salvation in your life

- Loving God with your whole desire puts you in close proximity to experience the desires in your heart

A Call To Action

Wisdom is key to living in God's kingdom. We are challenged to seek the kingdom of God daily. Growing in wisdom comes with understanding and knowledge to build your spiritual house in God's kingdom.

It's God's will that you conform to Jesus' image while living God's divine plan for your life. God will give you the wisdom needed to be who you were created to be. Simply ask God to give you wisdom. James 1:5 (KJV) says, "If any of you lack wisdom, let him ask of God, that giveth to all men liberally, and upbraideth not; and it shall be given him." God will give you wisdom for every area of your life.

Pray the following prayer:

Lord,
I ask that you give me the wisdom to be all you created me to be. I receive your instruction and knowledge to grow in wisdom. I ask that my creativity expands in my talent, skills, and abilities. That I know how to use my time for prayer, meditation, planning, and taking action. Most important that my time is in harmony with living my purpose. I receive that I am rewarded for spiritual growth, investments, sacrifice, hard work, persistence, time, and betting on myself. Thank you for giving me wisdom. In Jesus Name

Meditate
Read and Meditate on Proverbs 8.

Chapter 9

Vision

"And the LORD answered me, and said, Write the vision,
and make it plain upon tables, that
he may run that readeth it."

Habakkuk 2:2 (KJV)

I sat on the floor, creating a vision board. I created it with much thought regarding my spiritual life, relationships, career, finances, health, leisure, etc. I must tell you 80 percent of what was in the vision remains on the vision board. This vision board was created four years ago. It didn't represent God's plans for my life. I no longer desire what I put on the board. I created it based on my own understanding. I didn't seek God.

This chapter is about receiving God's vision for your life. A vision from God is connected to who you were created to be in Christ and God's plans for your life. It's important to know and understand a vision from God. A vision is a revelation. Revelation is what is revealed to you in God's Word. God uses his word to create a vision. God's word has promises from the books of Genesis to Revelation. God's promises for your life are confirmed in the Bible.

A vision from God starts with a problem. God looked at the earth and saw a problem. God saw the earth was chaotic and disorganized. Genesis 1:2 (KJV) says, "And the earth was without form, and void; and darkness was upon the face of the deep. And the Spirit of God moved upon the face of the waters." The Spirit of God moved with will and determination to create order in the earth. God's vision for the earth was order. This vision started with God's word. Genesis 1:3 (KJV) says, "And God said, 'Let there be light:' and there was light." God's spoken word for the earth was light. This light is the source from which all things were created. God created you in his image and likeness to create your life with his word. God's answers to your life problems and success is a vision that comes from his word.

A vision from God shows up in conflict, sorrow, tension, stress, pain, adversity, debt, controversy, failures, injustice, etc. Habakkuk, Prophet of God, witnessed injustice, destruction, violence, strife, conflict in his nation. Habakkuk Chapter 1 provides a description of Habakkuk's experience and communication to God. He questioned God about the chaos in his nation. Habakkuk 1:3 (NIV) says, "Why do you make me look at injustice? Why do you tolerate wrongdoing? Destruction and violence are before me; there is strife, and conflict abounds." Habakkuk wanted to know why God was being tolerant of the injustice.

Habakkuk's communication to God was prayer. He had focused prayer with God. Habakkuk 2:1 (KJV) says, "I will stand upon my watch, and set me upon the tower, and will watch to see what he will say unto me, and what I shall answer when I am reproved." Habakkuk waited on God's response. God response was to write a vision. Habakkuk 2:2 (KJV) says, "And the LORD answered me, and said, Write the vision, and make it plain upon tables, that he may run that readeth it."

A vision from God reveals to you the life God planned for you to experience.

A Vision From God:	Is God's word revealed to you
	Should be written down
	Leads to clarity
	Is a call to action
	Motivates you
	Has an appointed time
	Is a solution
	Requires patience
	Guarantee Success

Your Vision from God Removes Oppression and Bondage

God's word/vision removes oppression and bondage in your life. Jeremiah 23:29 (KJV) says, "Is not my word like as a fire? saith the LORD; and like a hammer that breaketh the rock in pieces?" Oppression and bondage are anything that keep you from living the desires in your heart. What has you confused? What has your back against the wall? What part of your life is chaotic and disorganized? What brings you to tears? God sees it and will respond to you.

You may be thinking that if God sees it, why hasn't he changed the situation. God created you in his image and likeness to have dominion over your life. This includes giving you the vision to move past any oppression and bondage. You have dominion over life circumstances. You may say, "I prayed, and nothing happened."

The circumstances you experience in your life are symptoms. God's word deal with the root of your circumstances. Jesus saw a fig tree showed symptoms of not producing figs in the right season. The root of the fig tree caused the tree to be abnormal. Jesus spoke words to the fig tree to deal with the problems. Mark 11:14 (KJV) says, "And Jesus answered and said unto it, 'No man eat fruit of thee hereafter for ever.' And his disciples heard it." The words Jesus spoke caused the fig tree to wither and die from the roots. Mark 11:20 (KJV) says, "And in the morning, as they passed by, they saw the fig tree dried up from the roots."

The roots to your life issues keeps you from growing into the fullness of who you were created to be in Christ, while living God's plans for your life. This is a life Jesus chose and appointed you to live. You remain disconnected from God's word when you don't choose the life Jesus chose and appointed you to live. John 15:5 (KJV) says, "I am the vine, ye are the branches: He that abideth in me, and I in him, the same bringeth forth much fruit: for without me ye can do nothing." The circumstances in your life are results of being disconnected to your source of living. God's vision for your life connects you to the desires in your heart.

Remember: The foundation for the desires of your heart are:

1. Being who you were created to be in Christ

2. God's plans for your life

God's vision speaks to the roots of oppression and bondage in your life. Oppression and bondage are mountains in your life. They are smokescreens that cause you to believe and think you aren't equipped or worthy of living the desires in your heart.

Therefore, it's important to believe that God's word is your truth to live by. God's vision works in your life when you believe in him. Jesus acknowledged that mountains are removed from your life when you don't doubt his word in your heart. Jesus said in Mark 11:23 (KJV), "For verily I say unto you, That whosoever shall say unto this mountain, Be thou removed, and be thou cast into the sea; and shall not doubt in his heart, but shall believe that those things which he saith shall come to pass; he shall have whatsoever he saith." Not doubting God's vision for your life creates a path to experience desires in your heart. Jesus said in Mark 11:24 (KJV), "Therefore I say unto you, 'What things soever ye desire, when ye pray, believe that ye receive them, and ye shall have them." God grants you the desires of your heart when you receive and act on the vision he has for your life.

How to Identify Your Vision from God

Sarah Breedlove, known as Madame CJ Walker, was a successful self-made millionaire. She was born on a Louisiana plantation on December 23, 1867 and became an orphan at age seven. Harvard Business School conducted a case study on Walker's entrepreneur success.

In the article, *HBS Cases: Beauty Entrepreneur Madam Walker*, written by Martha Lagace, Nancy F Koehn, and Katherine Miller from Harvard Business School, it explained what motivated Madam CJ Walker.

Professor Koehn observed how Madam CJ Walker moved past complex adversities as an African-American woman. Koehn said, "She lived on a fascinating threshold between the end of slavery, the beginnings of the great migration northward by African Americans, and the opening up of consumer capitalism." Professor Koehn observed during the case study that Madam CJ Walker found her way to success with her vision and business model. According to Madam CJ Walker's biographer and great-great Granddaughter A' Lelia Bundles, Walker suffered from a scalp ailment that caused her to lose most of her hair. Her scalp ailment caused her to create a formula to treat the scalp.

In *Madam Walker's Essay*, by A' Lelia Bundles, Bundles said, "After changing her name to 'Madam' C. J. Walker, she founded her own business and began selling Madam Walker's Wonderful Hair Grower, a scalp conditioning and healing formula, which she claimed had been revealed to her in a dream." Bundles said, "Tenacity and perseverance, faith in herself and in God, quality products and 'honest business dealings' were the elements and strategies she prescribed for aspiring entrepreneurs who requested the secret to her rags-to-riches ascent."

Madam CJ Walker told a reporter the following:

"God answered my prayer, for one night I had a dream, and in that dream, a big black man appeared to me and told me what to mix up for my hair. Some of the remedy is grown in Africa, but I sent for it, mixed it, put it on my scalp, and in a few weeks, my hair was coming in faster than it had ever fallen out. I tried it on my friends, and it helped them. I made up my mind I would begin to sell it."

It's evident that Madam CJ Walker had a vision from God. This is the same for you; God has and will reveal his vision to you.

God's vision for your life is connected to his plans for your life. God is seeking to give you a vision now. His vision for your life will come in the form of an idea. Madam CJ Walker had an idea to create a scalp formula. Ideas come to your mind daily. You must recognize the ones that come from God. The ideas come in the midst of a problem. Madam CJ Walker suffered hair loss. This was a problem God gave Walker the ability to solve.

Answer the following questions:

What problem are you experiencing now?
What idea came to your mind that is connected to the problem?

The idea God gives you is connected to your freedom in Christ. Ideas from God gives you the opportunity to be who you were created to be. This is the place where God is offering you the opportunity to experience his divine nature.

God's spirit moves over ideas that come with freedom for you. 2 Corinthians 3:17 (KJV) says, "Now the Lord is that Spirit: and where the Spirit of the Lord is, there is liberty."

I mentioned earlier in the chapter that the chaotic and disorganized state of the earth caused God to move upon the waters in the earth. God has the solution in ideas for circumstances that breed chaos. I was sitting in my office at the high school in deep thought regarding the problems students were experiencing. God gave me the idea to start a mentoring group. Life circumstances may have flooded your life where you can't think clearly to hear from God. I challenge you to make time to hear from God. This includes thinking about ideas God is seeking to express through you. Thinking is the place where God expresses his thoughts for your life. Psalm 92:5 (KJV) says, "O LORD, how great are thy works! and thy thoughts are very deep."

God shares his deep thoughts when you contemplate his word through meditation. I prayed in 2018 for clarity regarding God's plans for my life. This was a process because God was taking away my limited thinking in exchange for his thoughts regarding the desires in my heart. I received clarity at the end of the year. This came by me taking the time to meditate on God's word. I went into deep thinking, connecting the dots regarding God's plans for my life. I would have quit this process if I didn't have the knowledge of how deep thinking works. You should consider the following when ideas come to your mind:

1. How is the idea connected to your talent?
2. How is the idea connected to your influence?
3. How is the idea connected to your potential?
4. How is the idea connected to your strengths?
5. What can you do within your control to test the idea?

Continue to pray over the idea and ask God to confirm it in his word. God's word will give you faith for the idea. Your faith will give you the assurance that God breathed life on this idea. The following question is to identify how God's word is connected to the idea:

How does the idea promote God's kingdom?

Ideas from God comes with responsibility. The responsibility is to communicate your Christian lifestyle. This is a commandment from Jesus.

Jesus said in Matthew 28:19-20 (NIV), "Therefore go and make disciples of all nations, baptizing them in the name of the Father and of the Son and of the Holy

Spirit, [20] and teaching them to obey everything I have commanded you. And surely I am with you always, to the very end of the age." This is the "Great Commission" for everyone who believes Jesus is Lord and Savior. God's vision for your life comes with the opportunity for you to promote the mind of Christ. This is your platform. Frances Ellen Watkins Harper said, "Jesus Christ has given us a platform of life and duty from which all oppression and selfishness is necessarily excluded."

Amanda Riggan said, "Be Jesus with skin on." Amanda started Hungry Heroes, a non-profit organization that serves food to first responders. A tragic event occurred for police officers in her community, and she was thinking about how she could serve first responders. Amanda said, "It just came to me to feed them." God gave her the idea to feed first responders. "When the Lord is pulling on your heart strings, do you move your feet?" said Amanda in response to God giving her an idea. Your vision from God includes serving humanity. This is connected to God giving you the power to be wealthy. Deuteronomy 8:18 (KJV) says, "But thou shalt remember the LORD thy God: for it is he that giveth thee power to get wealth, that he may establish his covenant which he sware unto thy fathers, as it is this day."

God's vision for you is to become wealthy. This starts with being wealthy in your image, talent, and influence. God empowers you to be wealthy, so he can establish his covenant on the earth. One of many definitions of covenant is agreement of the mind. God created you to be in oneness with him to establish his thoughts and ways on the earth. You express God's thoughts through your authentic image, talent, and influence. Christianity is about serving and expressing God's love towards all people. Your service in God's love is attached to God's vision for your life. This involves knowing where your influence is needed. There are cultural mountains followers of Christ are to serve and express God's love.

According to *7culturalmountains.org*, there are seven cultural spheres Christians are called to influence with their talent, skills, and abilities. The seven cultural mountains are arts and entertainment, business, education, family, government, media, and spirituality. Isaiah 2:2 (KJV) says, "And it shall come to pass in the last days, that the mountain of the LORD's house shall be established in the top of the mountains, and shall be exalted above the hills; and all nations shall flow unto it."

God's desire is to bring hope to cultures by influencing people to be consciously aware of their oneness with him. God individually gave Bill Bright and Loren Cunningham the vision for Christians to influence seven cultures. Bright and Cunningham met in 1975 and confirmed with one another the vision God gave them. You can identify how each cultural mountain needs solutions. You are called to one or more of the cultural mountains. Your influence is connected to solving problems.

God's vision for your life includes solving problems for people with your influence. OS Hillman, founder of 7culturalmountains.org, said, "Influence is a result of our love, humility, and obedience to God, not a goal to be achieved." Answer the following questions:

1. Which cultural mountain are you called to influence?
2. How will you use your influence to provide a solution?
3. How will you build your influence in your current environment? Example: Career

It is IMPORTANT when you receive a vision from God; you take the following action:

- Believe God

- Receive it by faith
- Don't doubt God in your heart
- Speak God's Word
- Act on God's word

"Influence is a result of our love, humility, and obedience to God, not a goal to be achieved."
-OS Hillman

I challenge you to journal your ideas that come to your mind. The idea may seem vague in the beginning, but clarity comes when you remain in faith without doubting the vision. In Acts Chapter 10, Peter was praying to God and went into a trance. God gave Peter a vision, which Peter doubted the meaning. Peter continued to think about the vision. Acts 10:19 (KJV) says, "While Peter thought on the vision, the Spirit said unto him, Behold, three men seek thee."

Clarity of the vision came to Peter when he continued to think about it. Peter realized with clarity that God was instructing him to meet with three men. Acts 10:20 (KJV) says, "Arise, therefore, and get thee down, and go with them, doubting nothing: for I have sent them." God will instruct you when you make room for his vision in your heart. Please, don't ignore visions from God. This is your path to freedom. Instead, pray about the vision. Think about the vision. Receive God's instructions about the vision.

"When the Lord is pulling on your heart strings, do you move your feet?"
–Amanda Riggan

When you receive God's instructions, I challenge you to do the following:

1. Take Action

Discovering and living the desires of the heart comes with a spiritual lifestyle in Christ. This is about having a relationship with God while resting with the mind of Christ and growing in wisdom. This will require your faith and action. Desires of the heart include experiencing your oneness with God. You and God partnering to serve and express God's love for humanity. Partnership is based on agreement. God is looking for you to agree with him in your mind. This creates the opportunity for you to walk with him. Amos 3:3 (KJV) says, "Can two walk together, except they be agreed?"

One definition of walk is to live, act or behave. This includes making the choice to choose a certain course of life. Jesus said in John 14:6 (KJV), "I am the way, the truth, and the life: no man cometh unto the Father, but by me." Jesus is the way, truth, and life to you being who you were created to be while living God's plans for your life. Jesus is the legal way to experiencing the desires in your heart.

God will give you a vision to put into action. This comes with God's instructions. Your desires expand as you put into action God's vision for your life. I challenge you not to hesitate. Take action by faith. God's spirit creates open doors of opportunity for you to profit from the vision. This is a form of being obedient to God. Isaiah 1:19 (KJV) says, "If ye be willing and obedient, ye shall eat the good of the land:" You experience the goodness of your works when you conform to the image of Jesus by being obedient to the talent, influence and vision God place in your heart.

This will cause God to open his hand and satisfy the desire "to be" more in your heart. To live in the fullness of your divine nature in Christ. This comes when you take action to discover and live the desires of your heart through a spiritual lifestyle in Christ by faith.

Chapter 9 Summary

- A vision from God is connected to who you were created to be in Christ and God's plans for your life
- God uses his word to create a vision for your life
- A vision from God shows up in conflict, sorrow, tension, stress, pain, adversity, debt, controversy, failures, injustice, etc.
- God's word/vision removes oppression and bondage in your life
- God vision for your life will come in the form of an idea
- The idea God gives you is connected to your freedom in Christ
- According to 7culturalmountains.org, there are seven cultural spheres Christians are called to influence with their talent, skills, and abilities
- The seven cultural mountains are arts and entertainment, business, education, family, government, media, and spirituality
- It is IMPORTANT when you receive a vision from God; you take the following action:

  1. Believe God

  2. Receive it by faith

  3. Don't doubt God in your heart

4. Speak God's Word

5. Act on God's word

A Call To Action

God has an idea for you that is connected to your freedom in Christ. Some people call it a God idea. Your idea from God comes with independent thinking without logic and reasoning.

How will you respond to an idea from God?

A God idea may appear insignificant. It will come at a time when your plate is full of commitments. This is your test. You pass the test by acting on the idea. The idea will come. Hebrews 4:7 (KJV) says, "To day if ye will hear his voice, harden not your hearts."

Pray the following prayer:

Lord,

I recognize your vision for my life is connected to my freedom in Christ. I open my heart to you by receiving your divine influence on my heart. I ask that you reveal to me the ideas you have set aside for me. I choose to use my time to pray and seek you with all my heart. Your word says, **"The LORD confides in those who fear him; he makes his covenant known to them."** (Psalm 25:14 NIV). Thank you for making your covenant known to me by confiding your ideas in my heart. I affirm I will put into action the ideas God places in my heart. In Jesus Name.

Meditate

Read and Meditate on Habakkuk 2:2-3 and Jeremiah 29:11-14

Daily Affirmations

I am made in God's image and likeness.

Genesis 1:27

I am chosen and ordained to be productive in spirit and truth.

John 15:16

Holy Spirit guides me into all truth.

John 16:13

God's word is my truth. I am sanctified by God's word.

John 17:17

I have the mind of Christ.

I Corinthians 2:16

I live my vision from God.

Habakkuk 2:2

I own my truth.

Proverbs 23:23

My spiritual foundation stands on the word of God.

Luke 6:47-48

I have wisdom, understanding, and knowledge to live in the fullness of God's image.

Proverbs 24:3-4

I am influential and impactful in the culture God called me to serve.

Matthew 28: 19-20

I use my God given talent with excellence, service, and profit.

Matthew 25:15-17

I have talent, skills, and abilities in wisdom, understanding, and knowledge.

Exodus 35:31

God teaches how to use my talent.

Exodous 4:15

I am growing strong in spirit filled with wisdom in God's grace.

Luke 2:40

Notes

Introduction

1. James Allen, *As A Man Thinketh*-Authorized Edition, (Middletown, DE 2016) 1
2. Douglas Aumack and Anna Aschkenes, "Behind The Scenes.." County of Middlesex Cultural and Heritage Commission, April 2, 2014, Access April 3, 2019, http://www.middlesexcountynj.gov/Government/Departme nts/BDE/Documents/Keckley%20bookletFinal.pdf

1. Desires of the Heart

1. Gallup Analytics, "State of the American Workplace Report" Gallup, 2016, Access March 22, 2017, https://news.gallup.com/reports/199961/7.aspx

2. Life

1. James Macintyre, "'God Just Came Into My Heart One Afternoon': The Extraordinary Life Of George Washington Carver, Christian Today, January 5, 2017 Access February 8, 2018, https://www.christiantoday.com/article/god-just-came-into-my-heart-one-afternoon-the-extraordinary-life-of-george-washington-carver/103618.htm

3. Rest

1. Matthew 11:28-30 (MSG)

4. Trust God

1. "Edification." Webster Dictionary 1828-Online Edition. http://webstersdictionary1828.com/Dictionary/Edification

5. Law of Human Nature

1. John Piper, "Out of Your Heart Will Flow Rivers of Living Water" Desiringgod.org, February 20, 2011, Access February 5, 2019, https://www.desiringgod.org/messages/out-of-your-heart-will-flow-rivers-of-living-water
2. "Imagination." Webster Dictionary 1828-Online Edition. http://webstersdictionary1828.com/Dictionary/Imagination
3. Joshua Parker, "Our Beginning" https://www.parkersmaple.com/pages/our-story

6. The Mind of Christ

1. Dan Peterson, "Bad Sports Behavior Starts In Youth" Livescience.com, December 8, 2008, https://www.livescience.com/3123-bad-sports-behavior-starts-youth.html

2. Scott Stump, "Millionaire uses fortune to help kids in struggling town" Today.com, April 17, 2013, https://www.today.com/news/millionaire-uses-fortune-help-kids-struggling-town-1C9373666

7. The Law of the Spirit of Life in Christ Jesus

1. Romans 8 (KJV)

8. Grow in Wisdom

1. Proverbs 8 (KJV)

9. Vision

1. Martha Lagace, "HBS Cases: Beauty Entrepreneur Madam Walker", Harvard Business School Working Knowledge, June 25, 2007, https://hbswk.hbs.edu/item/hbs-cases-beauty-entrepreneur-madam-walker

2. A'Lelia Bundles, "**Madam C.J. Walker: A Brief Biographical Essay** ©", madamcjwalker.com, http://www.madamcjwalker.com/bios/madam-c-j-walker/

3. Steve Harvey, "A Delivery Woman Who Offers Prayer", Stevetv.com, http://stevetv.com/story/a-delivery-woman-who-offers-a-prayer/

4. Amanda Riggan, Hungry Heroes, https://www.hungryheroesbbq.com/

ABOUT THE AUTHOR

Tulani Person is a life strategist, speaker, and author. She provides strategies for people to grow spiritually in Jesus Christ. Tulani worked close to 18 years for the State of Michigan when she discovered she was living a life of existing. She made plans to change careers and serve professional athletes as a life coach. God interrupted her plans. Tulani discovered her hidden desire to empower people to be who they were created to be. Including, living God's plans for their life.

Tulani is a certified speaker, trainer, and coach through the John Maxwell Team. Currently, she serves on John Maxwell Team's President Advisory Council.

Tulani is married to her loving husband Dale. She is the mother of two lovely daughters, Kristian and Dayla.

To book Tulani Person for speaking engagements, email tulaniperson@iamtulaniperson.com.

Made in the USA
Monee, IL
01 November 2020

46470146R00163